DO NOT REMOVE
CARDS FROM POCKET

ATLAS OF ECONOMIC ISSUES

ATLAS OF ECONOMIC ISSUES

DR. BILL MACMILLAN

Lecturer in Human Geography and
Fellow of Hertford College
Oxford University

DR. GORDON FELL

Mortimer May Research Scholar
Hertford College
Oxford University

Facts On File
New York • Oxford • Sydney

Library of Congress Cataloging-in-Publication Data
Macmillan, Bill.
    Atlas of economic issues/Bill Macmillan, Gordon Fell.
        p. cm.––(World contemporary issues)
    Includes index.
    ISBN 0–8160–2481–2
    1. Economics –– Juvenile literature. 2. Comparative economics –– Juvenile literature. 3. Economic history –– 1945 –– Juvenile literature. I. Fell. Gordon. II. Title. III. Series.
    HB183.M33 1991
    330 –– dc20   91-23433
                                                                          CIP

ISBN 0–8160–2481–2

Facts On File books are available at special discounts when purchased in bulk quantities for businesses, associations, institutions or sales promotions. Please call our Special Sales Department in New York at 212/683-2244 (dial 800/322–8755 except in NY, AK or HI).

An Ilex book

Created and produced by Ilex Publishers Limited
29–31 George Street, Oxford OX1 2AJ

Designed by John Downes and Simon Taylor

Illustrated by Janos Marffy and Mike Saunders/Jillian Burgess Illustration, Sailesh Thakrar and John Downes

Typesetting by Meridian Phototypesetting Ltd.
Color separations by Scantrans Pte. Ltd.
Printed in Spain

10 9 8 7 6 5 4 3 2 1

This book is printed on acid-free paper.

Contents

1 An Imaginary Economy

Imagine you have been shipwrecked on a deserted island. You are not alone; one of your friends has managed to get ashore with you in a small lifeboat. Having survived the wreck you must now survive on the island. You know you were a long way off any trade routes when the ship went down, so you may never be rescued. The island is quite large, mostly covered in trees, but with a few open spaces. There are birds and animals on the island and fish in the sea around it.

You would be faced with some very difficult questions. What will you do to ensure your survival? How will you do it? How will you share the burdens and rewards of life on the island? These are all *economic* questions. Indeed, similar questions have to be solved by every society. The great *economic issues* of today are all concerned, in one way or another, with the difficulties and conflicts involved in answering such questions.

Sharing burdens and rewards

Another basic question to be faced concerns the sharing of burdens and rewards. With so many jobs to be done, there are likely to be advantages from a division of labor. If you both do the jobs you are best at, you will be more productive than if you share every task equally. If you specialize though, it makes it more difficult to decide whether or not both of you are doing your fair share. As well as the problem of sharing the work load, you will also have to decide how to share the products of that work. Decisions about the allocation of burdens and rewards are major aspects of the social organization of your island economy. If one of you decided to claim the bulk of the output and make the other do the bulk of the work, you would have something like a slave economy. A form of organization regarded as generally 'fair,' would be easier to sustain, and may well be much more productive. The last basic economic decision then, after *what* to produce and *how* to produce it, is *who* to produce it for.

Basic human needs

First and foremost, you will be concerned with satisfying your basic needs and this may be quite a struggle. In many societies, this problem completely dominates people's lives. You will need fresh water, food and shelter. The most urgent problem is to find water. You could survive without food for several days but not without water. Suppose you are lucky enough to find a stream with fresh water which you trace back to a spring. Suppose there is also a small amount of fruit on trees near the spring. The immediate threats from thirst and starvation are lifted. What next? You will need shelter in the form of clothing and a dwelling of some

sort. You may also need protection from predators, such as animals or, perhaps, other humans. You will certainly need to protect yourself as far as possible from disease and a sensible sewerage facility would help.

To meet basic human needs, you have to create a sort of envelope around yourself, with enough water and food, not too much wind, rain and sun, and minimum contact with predators and disease organisms. The more successful you are, the more comfortable you will be. Your ability to succeed depends on the resources that are available and your ability to use them.

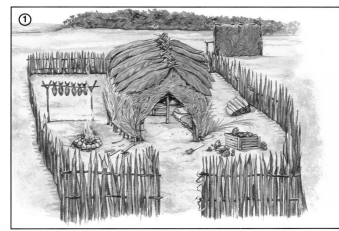

Consumption

The process of satisfying your needs and wants is called consumption. Water and food are consumer goods and so is shelter. What you consume depends on the consumption possibilities that are available to you and your preferences. If everything was so abundant on the island that you could have anything you wanted, only your preferences would matter. But let us suppose that the island is like the rest of the world in that many of the things you require are unavailable or in short supply. You will then be faced with the problem of scarcity – the fundamental problem in economics. To relieve this problem you will have to work. You will also have to budget; that is, you will have to decide how to 'spend' your time on various jobs.

Production

Although there are some things on the island that you can consume or utilize immediately, there are many things you will have to produce. Production requires inputs and yields outputs. There are three types of inputs: labor, capital, and land (including materials found in and on the land). Labor involves both physical strength, and physical and mental skills. Your own body is likely to be the only source of energy on the island that can be used easily. Capital goods are things like tools and pieces of equipment. The capital goods you have available constitute your

technology. What you can produce depends on what resources you have available. There are two of you who can work perhaps eight hours a day, the lifeboat and its equipment, and the island's material resources. You might spend your time hunting; you might use the boat for fishing; you might take the time to adapt things from the boat to use as tools and farming implements. There are, in short, various production possibilities. Basic questions about the ways and means of survival can now be thought of as the economic issues of *what* to produce and *how* to produce it.

2 Real Economies

Suppose you are rescued from the desert island by a passing ship which takes you to the nearest port. Safe at last! Or are you? How will you survive here in the port city? Your basic needs are the same as they were on the island but the opportunities for satisfying them are very different. The city has water on tap and many different kinds of food and shelter. It has much more besides – luxuries as well as necessities. To get almost anything though, you will require money (see MONEY AND ASSETS). In the city as on the island, survival requires work. In the city, though, work and survival are not connected directly. They are connected via the labor market and the food, housing and other markets. Your chances depend on how well you can operate in various markets and how well the markets operate for you.

A whole host of economic issues can be understood in part by thinking of them in these personal terms, but to understand them fully it is necessary to approach them in a more general way and to look at evidence on a regional, national or international scale. This Atlas focuses on three overlapping groups of issues. Using the theme of survival, the first group examines problems of development and underdevelopment (pages 32-41). This group merges into a second which deals with the domestic economic issues that concern rich and poor alike (pages 42-49). The third group deals with international economic issues (pages 50-61).

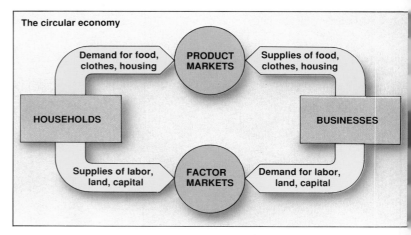

The circular economy

The circular economy

In a market economy HOUSEHOLDS supply LABOR to BUSINESSES via the job market and receive wages in return. Some households also supply land and invest money. To persuade people to invest money, businesses undertake to pay it back with interest. For the use of land, they pay rent. The levels of wages, rent and interest in this simplified picture are determined by supply and demand in the labor, land and money markets. In reality GOVERNMENT, trade unions, international institutions and other bodies have a role to play in this process. Businesses use the factors of production (labor, land and capital) obtained via the markets to produce products. These are sold to households at prices determined by the interaction of supply and demand in the product markets. Commodities (labor, land, capital and products) flow clockwise round the diagram, while the payments would flow counterclockwise.

Types of economic organization

The description of the port city on this page indicates that it is a *market economy* in which the questions of what to produce, how to produce and for whom to produce are answered by individual economic agents (businesses and households) interacting through markets. In practice, market economies are also capitalist economies. *Capitalism* involves the private ownership of the means of production. The United States, Canada, Western European countries and Japan are all predominantly capitalist. The state owns some industries in each of these countries. In the United Kingdom, for example, the railways are state owned, which means they are run, indirectly, by the government. Because of this, countries like the UK are said to be *mixed economies*. The revolution in Russia in 1917 ushered in a rival economic system – *soviet communism* – under which the state owns the means of production and the economy is planned centrally. This system has now collapsed in Eastern Europe and is unraveling in the old Soviet Union.

Work

In the city, as on the island, you will need to work to survive. What sort of work is there? One way of answering this question is to divide work up according to the type of thing that is being produced. The simplest way to do this is to talk about primary, secondary and tertiary activities. Primary activity includes AGRICULTURE, MINING and ENERGY production. Secondary activity is mainly MANUFACTURING. Manufactured goods include domestic ovens (an example of a consumer good) and car windshields (a producer good, since windshields are sold to other producers, in this case car manufacturers). Tertiary activity includes retailing, banking and other SERVICES, plus TRANSPORT AND COMMUNICATIONS. The bar chart (left) shows that primary activity tends to decrease in importance as countries get richer.

Sources and sizes of GDP, 1985

Industrial market economies

Middle income economies

Low income economies

Services

Industry

Agriculture

US $100 billion

Markets

A market is the name given to the trading arrangement for an economic good or service. Goods are physical products like cars and hot dogs. Services are things like haircuts and bus rides. Some commodities have a fixed market place but others, like housing and labor, do not. Sellers of a good or service try to earn as much as they can but if they set their price too high, buyers will go elsewhere.

Competition between sellers tends to make them fix their prices at about the same level. When there is just one seller in a market there is a monopoly. Monopolists can raise prices above the competitive level but if they fix them too high, people will look for substitute products instead. Indeed, nearly all prices are influenced by consumers' ability to substitute one thing for another – to buy pears instead of apples, or buy a bus ride instead of taking a taxi. The number of buyers in a market is important as well. In a town dominated by one employer, wage rates could be fixed at a lower level than if there was competition for labor. Roughly speaking, the more buyers and sellers there are, the more competition there will be.

Supply and demand

The price of a commodity tends to depend on supply (the amount available in the market) and demand (the amount that consumers want to buy). The higher the price of a commodity the more of it suppliers will want to sell, so supply tends to increase as the price increases. Conversely, the higher the price the less of the commodity consumers will want to buy, so demand tends to decrease as the price increases.

If the price is too high, supply will exceed demand. As a result, some of the commodity will remain unsold. There will be a surplus or excess supply.

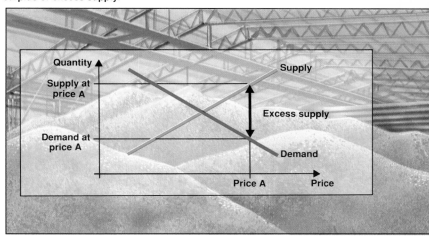

If the price is too low, demand will exceed supply. As a result, there will be shortages.

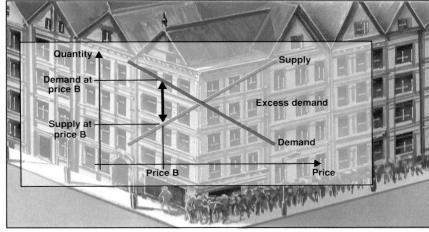

If the price is set at the right level, 'market clearing' will occur (no excess demand and no excess supply).

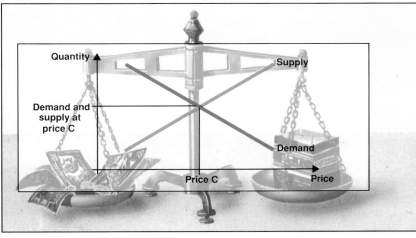

9

3 Money and Assets

Economies can function without money, and the basic activities of production and consumption can still occur (see AN IMAGINARY ECONOMY). In primitive economies, goods and services were swapped through the 'barter' system. This meant that a person who had a sheep and wanted a sack of wheat had to find someone who had wheat and wanted a sheep. Only then could the barter take place. As trade by barter was very inconvenient, most people tried to be self-sufficient by producing goods for their own consumption. This hindered economic development by preventing both specialized production and the linking of markets that were far apart. To overcome the problems of the barter system, a medium of exchange became necessary. This led to the development of money, which is now widely accepted in payment for goods and services. To boost economic activity, it must be portable, divisible and difficult to counterfeit.

Households and businesses accumulate wealth if they are able to earn more than they spend on goods and services. Wealth is held in the form of valuable assets. Money is one type of asset in an economy, while others are bonds, shares and real assets (see above right). The advantage of this second group of assets is that they often earn higher interest for the owner. The disadvantage is that they are not as easy to use as a means of payment. Households and businesses must decide how much of their wealth to hold as money and how much as other assets.

Money: Money includes both currency (notes and coins) in circulation and bank deposits from which money can be withdrawn at short notice.

Bonds: A bond is a promise by a borrower to pay a lender interest and repay the original loan on a specified date. Bonds are often used by governments to raise revenue.

Shares: A share is a claim to a share of the profits of a company. The stock exchanges that trade shares are now highly computerized.

Real assets: A real asset is a physical object of value, such as machines, buildings and land.

Problems with the barter system

A French singer gave a concert in the Society Islands in the late-19th century when the barter system was still used. Her payment was in pigs. turkeys. chickens and fruit. Perishable and difficult to transport home. the payment was both inconvenient and costly for Mademoiselle Zelie!

Saving, investment and the financial sector

Saving is simply the difference between income and consumption. For example, a household or business which earns $2,000 and spends $1,500 on goods and services is able to save $500. It then faces a decision about what to do with the saving. One possibility is to use the saving to finance household investments, such as the purchase of a house or car. This is called self-financing investment. On average households are able to finance all of their own investment from savings and have excess savings left over. Businesses generally do just the opposite.

The purpose of the financial sector is to transfer funds from economic units which save more than they invest, to those which invest more than they save. Without a financial system, only self-financing is possible. As a result, the economic plans formed by households, businesses and the government would be frustrated.

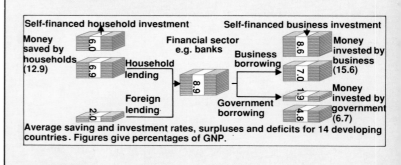

Self-financed household investment — Self-financed business investment

Money saved by households (12.9) — 6.0 — 6.9 — Household lending — Financial sector e.g. banks — 8.9 — Foreign lending — Business borrowing — Government borrowing — 8.6 — 7.0 — 1.9 — 4.8 — Money invested by business (15.6) — Money invested by government (6.7)

Average saving and investment rates, surpluses and deficits for 14 developing countries. Figures give percentages of GNP.

Printing money

Governments control the printing of money. Why then, do they not simply print more money to make everyone better off? Unfortunately, it is not as easy as it sounds. If the amount of money in the economy (the money supply) increases, then people, feeling richer, want to consume more goods and services. The higher demand leads to higher prices (see REAL ECONOMIES). The map shows that in countries where the money supply has grown rapidly, inflation (the rate of increase of prices) has also been high.

Average 'narrow money' growth (%)

- Over 50
- 20-50
- 10-20
- 5-10
- Less than 5
- Data not available

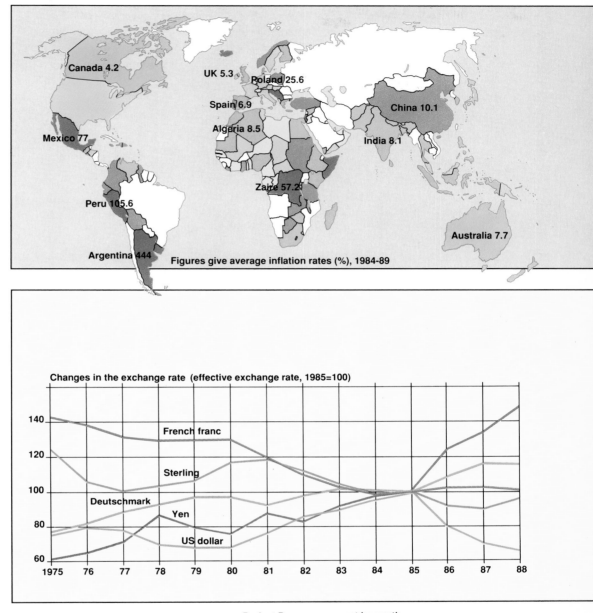

Canada 4.2
UK 5.3
Poland 25.6
Spain 6.9
China 10.1
Algeria 8.5
India 8.1
Mexico 77
Zaire 57.2
Peru 105.6
Australia 7.7
Argentina 444

Figures give average inflation rates (%), 1984-89

Exchange rates

The amount of one country's currency that can be bought with another country's currency is called the exchange rate. International trade depends heavily on exchange rates. If the value of a country's currency falls, then export from that country will be cheaper for other countries to buy. This is likely to increase the amount of exports demanded, so that exporters are in a more competitive position. However, the lower value of the currency also makes imports more expensive to buy and may increase the total amount spent on imports if the goods required cannot be drawn from local sources. Rapid changes in exchange rates make it difficult for businesses to plan profitable trade. Countries, therefore, may decide to link their exchange rate to a major currency. The members of the European Community have joined the Exchange Rate Mechanism, which fixes variations in exchange rates within agreed bands.

Changes in the exchange rate (effective exchange rate, 1985=100)

French franc
Sterling
Deutschmark
Yen
US dollar

1975 76 77 78 79 80 81 82 83 84 85 86 87 88

Interest rates and loans

When a loan is made, as with all economic transactions, each party receives a benefit and in return pays a cost. The price paid by the borrower for the use of the money is called 'interest', which the lender receives in return for no longer being able to spend the money immediately. Interest is usually calculated as a percentage of the amount borrowed. The level of interest rates is crucial to the economy. Businesses, households and the government decide whether to make new investments depending on the interest rate. Say a business wants to open a new factory. Its first step is to investigate the profitability of the project. The key question is whether profits from the sales of the goods produced by the factory exceed the payments on the loan necessary to make the investment. Suppose the interest rate is 10%, out of the three projects considered (see right) project A would certainly be worth pursuing: its rate of return is always greater than 10%.

Rate of return and interest rate

10%

A
B
C

Time

Project B may or may not be worth pursuing. In this case the time horizon (the life of the project) is crucial. Project C would not be worth pursuing.

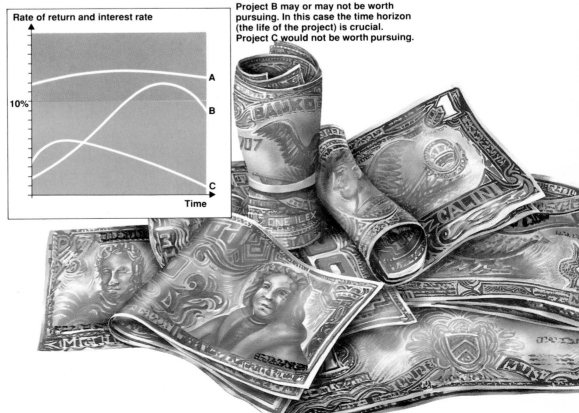

4 Agriculture

Agriculture is the dominant economic activity in most of the poorest parts of the world. The map (right) shows the percentage of total output (Gross Domestic Product) that comes from agriculture. The average for the industrialized market economies is less than 4% while for Sub-Saharan Africa, South Asia and the Asian Planned economies it is around 35%. What makes agriculture so important though, is not so much the contribution it makes to total output, but the share of total employment that it provides (see the map far right). In the industrialized market economies, about 8% of the work force is engaged in agriculture but in Sub-Saharan Africa, South Asia and the Asian Planned economies more than 65% make their living from the land. Compared with the industrialized economies, output per worker in these countries is very low (see the bar chart).

In developing countries, governments are confronted with many important agricultural issues. What can be done to improve productivity and output? How can old tenure systems be altered to give more people access to land? Should the production of cash crops be promoted to help earn the foreign currency that is required for vital imports or should food production for domestic consumption be the first priority?

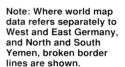

Note: Where world map data refers separately to West and East Germany, and North and South Yemen, broken border lines are shown.

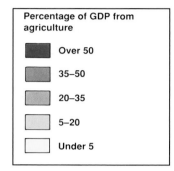

Percentage of GDP from agriculture

- Over 50
- 35–50
- 20–35
- 5–20
- Under 5

The Green Revolution
The introduction of new High Yielding Varieties (HYVs) of crops such as rice, wheat and corn from the mid-1960s was called the Green Revolution because it was thought that it would revolutionize agriculture in some of the world's poorest countries. However, the HYVs were only planted in some areas and, primarily, by the wealthiest farmers. By the mid-1970s it seemed that they had served only to widen rural inequalities. Modern evidence suggests that some of the early promise of the Green Revolution is starting to be fulfilled. Many new varieties of HYVs have been added which are suited to a wider range of environments and their use has spread from the wealthiest farmers to those with smaller farms and food production has increased dramatically.

The distribution of land
Ownership of land and access to it has been a central issue in revolution and social unrest, particularly as newly independent countries have tried to overturn colonial patterns of land distribution. Reform is also important if land is to be used in the most productive way to feed growing populations. Governments can either forcibly redistribute land, known as land reform, or encourage colonization of new areas. In either case, real gains can only be made if land redistribution is accompanied by improved transport links, credit facilities and better marketing networks.

Land reform in Brazil
Land reform is a pressing issue in Brazil, where the old colonial *hacienda* land-holding system has left large estates in the hands of only 300,000 powerful families. The government plans to buy 107 million acres from this class and resettle 7 million people on them, mainly in the northeast. The landowners are fighting these plans, arguing that there is plenty of spare land in Amazonia and in the southwest. In recent years there has been much violence between peasants trying to seize land and the landowners' private armies.

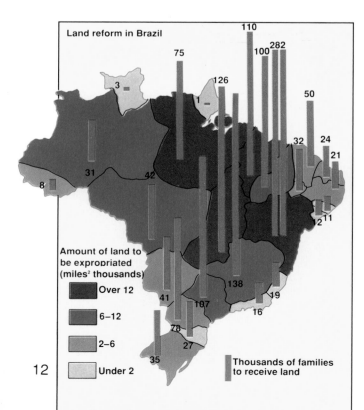

Land reform in Brazil

Amount of land to be expropriated (miles² thousands)

- Over 12
- 6–12
- 2–6
- Under 2

Thousands of families to receive land

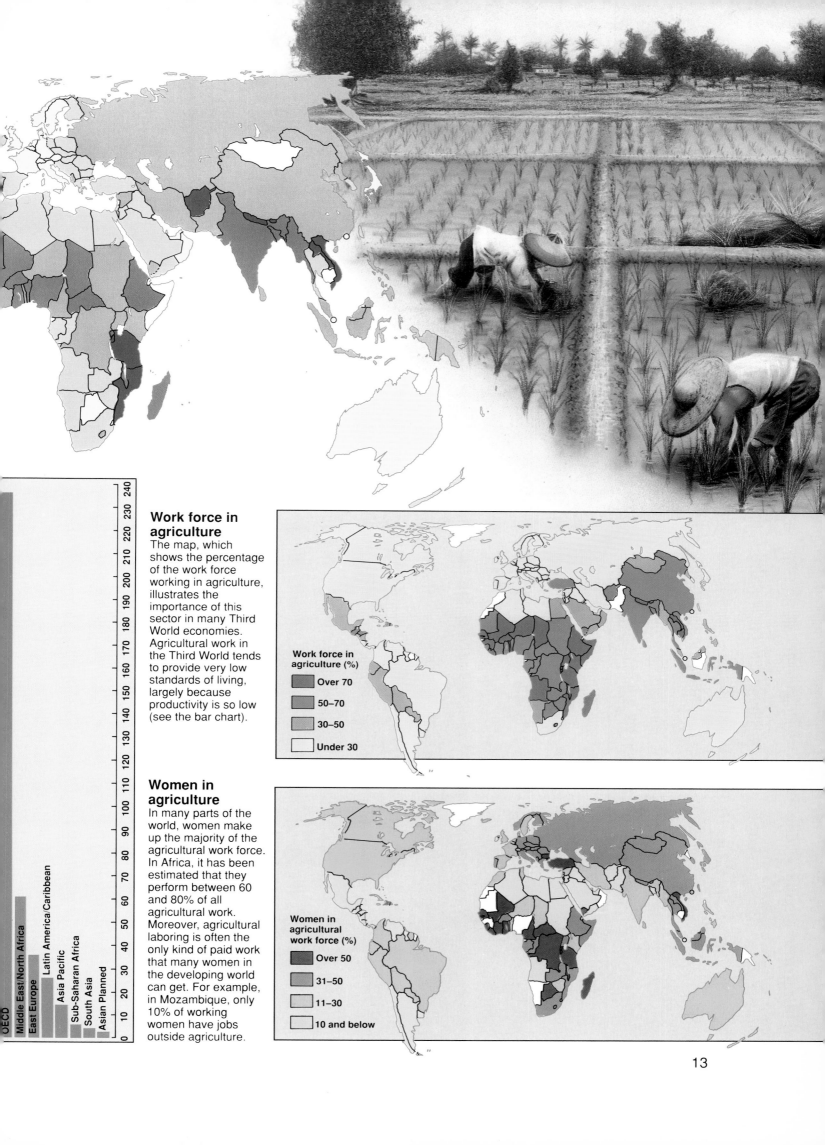

Work force in agriculture

The map, which shows the percentage of the work force working in agriculture, illustrates the importance of this sector in many Third World economies. Agricultural work in the Third World tends to provide very low standards of living, largely because productivity is so low (see the bar chart).

Work force in agriculture (%)

- Over 70
- 50–70
- 30–50
- Under 30

Women in agriculture

In many parts of the world, women make up the majority of the agricultural work force. In Africa, it has been estimated that they perform between 60 and 80% of all agricultural work. Moreover, agricultural laboring is often the only kind of paid work that many women in the developing world can get. For example, in Mozambique, only 10% of working women have jobs outside agriculture.

Women in agricultural work force (%)

- Over 50
- 31–50
- 11–30
- 10 and below

OECD
Middle East/North Africa
East Europe
Latin America/Caribbean
Asia Pacific
Sub-Saharan Africa
South Asia
Asian Planned

0 10 20 30 40 50 60 70 80 90 100 110 120 130 140 150 160 170 180 190 200 210 220 230 240

5 Mining

The minerals that lie beneath the Earth's surface are crucial to economic activity. They provide energy sources and raw materials used by industry.

Minerals form part of the non-renewable natural resource base of a country. In order to use minerals for industrial production, rocks containing the mineral (ore) must be extracted from the ground and processed to obtain the pure minerals. Various metallic minerals may then be combined to form alloys, such as steel. Often this last step may occur in countries which have very little mineral wealth themselves. For example, Japan imports large quantities of the raw materials required to make steel, and has built up an enormous steel industry.

The extraction and processing of minerals is costly, energy-intensive and requires technological expertise. Developing countries have extensive mineral deposits (see above, right) but rarely have the capacity to exploit them without help. The involvement of a multinational corporation is often necessary to finance a project and provide technological knowledge.

Mining Antarctica

Mining can cause great damage to the environment. Nowhere is the tension between economic and environmental factors better illustrated than in deciding whether or not to mine in Antarctica. According to the current theory of continental formation, Africa, Australia, Antarctica and South America were once connected to form an enormous southern continent called Gondwanaland. Mineral rich areas in South Africa and Australia were once attached to Antarctica, suggesting that substantial Antarctic deposits are likely. Deposits of iron ore and coal have already been found. Nevertheless, a decision was recently made to preserve Antarctica as a wilderness by banning mining for the next 50 years. The environmental costs were thought to outweigh the economic benefits of mining.

Stockpiles

Countries that rely on mineral imports need to ensure that minerals vital to their national interest, especially defense, are available. Their supply may be subject to disruption for political reasons and therefore many countries keep a reserve or 'stockpile' of important minerals.

US stockpiles

Bauxite 15,950,000 tons
Manganese 2,409,000 tons
Chromium 1,958,000 tons
Tin 203,500 tons
Cobalt 20,900 tons
Tantalum 699 tons
Palladium 1,380,500 ounces
Platinum 498,300 ounces

Coal mining in Colombia

The exploitation of mineral resources is an important aspect of many countries' development strategies. The Cerrejón North Coal Project is one of the world's biggest coal mines, set up as a joint venture between the Colombian government and Exxon (a multinational corporation involved in energy). The scale of the production and export complex is enormous. The mine has provided employment for local people, promoted some local businesses and generated new roads. In addition, Exxon's profits from the project are taxed as royalties which boost the revenue of the Colombian government. However, the project has been criticized as damaging the environment and harming a local nomadic people. Economically, the project has been condemned as serving Exxon's interests rather than Colombia's. This is a typical criticism of multinational corporations in developing countries, and is difficult to resolve. However, well-regulated mining ventures are probably the key to economic development in certain countries.

Coal from the mine at Cerrejón North being loaded onto ships

Major producers

The map shows that the developing countries have extensive deposits of many important minerals. Because of their high demand for minerals, many industrialized countries depend on imports from developing countries. The European Community is 70% dependent on mineral imports, including over 95% of its copper, chromium and manganese, most of which it obtains from developing countries. In order to ensure a secure supply of important minerals, the European Community signed an agreement, the Lome Convention, with 46 developing countries in 1975 to guarantee prices and amounts. For developing countries the revenue earned from mineral exports is vital to their economic development.

Mineral resources of the sea

The seabed contains vast amounts of minerals. The greatest potential source of minerals could be the many millions of manganese nodules which are thought to cover about a fifth of the ocean floor. The difficulty is to find a way of making their recovery profitable, which depends on technology and the availability of other sources. Another problem is the uncertainty as to who owns the mineral resources. Under an international agreement – the Law of the Sea – coastal countries now have the right to mine up to 200 nautical miles from their shores, but there is no agreement about deep-sea mining.

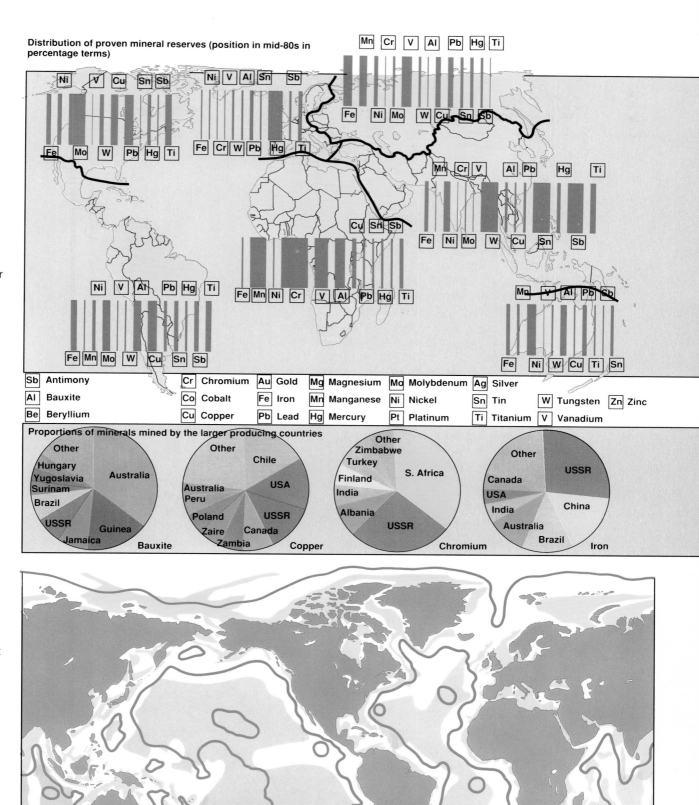

Distribution of proven mineral reserves (position in mid-80s in percentage terms)

Sb	Antimony	Cr	Chromium	Au	Gold	Mg	Magnesium	Mo	Molybdenum	Ag	Silver
Al	Bauxite	Co	Cobalt	Fe	Iron	Mn	Manganese	Ni	Nickel	Sn	Tin	W	Tungsten	Zn	Zinc
Be	Beryllium	Cu	Copper	Pb	Lead	Hg	Mercury	Pt	Platinum	Ti	Titanium	V	Vanadium

Proportions of minerals mined by the larger producing countries

Bauxite: Other, Hungary, Yugoslavia, Surinam, Brazil, USSR, Jamaica, Guinea, Australia

Copper: Other, Chile, USA, USSR, Canada, Zambia, Zaire, Poland, Australia, Peru

Chromium: Other, Zimbabwe, Turkey, Finland, India, Albania, USSR, S. Africa

Iron: Other, USSR, Canada, USA, India, Australia, Brazil, China

Manganese nodule distribution: The mineral content of the nodules is as high as any quality ore found on land.

Potential hydrocarbon basins: Currently, 20% of the world's oil production comes from beneath the sea.

Limit of Exclusive Economic Zones

15

6 Energy

Everyone needs energy. As consumers, we use a lot of energy in the form of electricity, and this has to be generated, that is, it has to be produced from some energy source. Ultimately, energy comes from the Sun but most of the sources we use contain solar energy in a fossilized form. This applies to the world's three major energy sources – coal, oil and natural gas (see the pie chart, bottom right). The process of fossilization takes so long we can think of these sources of energy as being non-renewable because we can use them up. There are, however, other energy sources which are essentially renewable. The three kinds of renewable energy that are used extensively are: biomass (plant and animal matter that can be converted into fuel), hydropower and nuclear power. In some of the world's poorest countries more than 90% of the energy consumed is biomass energy in the form of fuelwood. It is very difficult to estimate just how much of the world's energy supply comes from this source but it is probably around 20% and rising.

Different sources of energy have different properties. They vary, for example, in their cleanliness and in the hazards associated with their use. Of the main three sources, oil is the most attractive for many purposes: it is indispensable for road vehicles and aircraft; it is cleaner than coal for power generation; and it is easier to transport than natural gas. Indeed oil is by far the most widely traded of all commodities; more oil is traded by weight than the next three most-traded commodities (iron ore, coal and grain) combined.

Trade in oil, 1989
(million barrels per year)

Fuelwood scarcity in the developing countries

■ Acute scarcity: not even a minimum supply available

□ Deficit: fuelwood resources below requirements

The spread of radioactive gases from Chernobyl

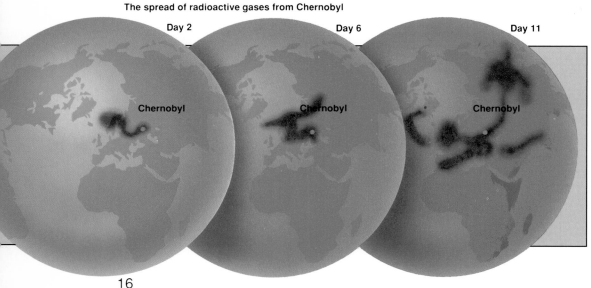

Day 2   Day 6   Day 11

Chernobyl   Chernobyl   Chernobyl

Energy hazards
Some energy technologies are safer than others but all major sources of energy have risks of some kind associated with them. The Chernobyl disaster in the Soviet Union in 1986 was the world's worst nuclear accident. It will be many years before its full effects are known. The radioactive cloud caused by the explosion at Chernobyl eventually spread as far as Canada, Africa, Pakistan and Korea. Hydroelectric power is thought of as a safe and clean technology. However, dams can fail with disastrous consequences. In 1889 the failure of the South Fork Dam in Johnstown, Pennsylvania, USA killed more than 2,000 people.

Soviet Union

1,100

Japan

dle t

939

Asia

309

Fuelwood shortages

The term 'energy crisis' has been used in the Western world to describe the problems caused by rises in the price of oil. This problem has affected less developed countries too, and very badly in some cases. But many of these countries have yet another energy crisis to contend with which is every bit as serious. This is the fuelwood crisis. In Mali, 97% of energy consumption comes from fuelwood. In Chad and Burkina Faso, the figure is 94%. Fuelwood is used mainly for cooking and heating. In rural areas, many villages that were once surrounded by forests now have expanding rings of desolate country around them.

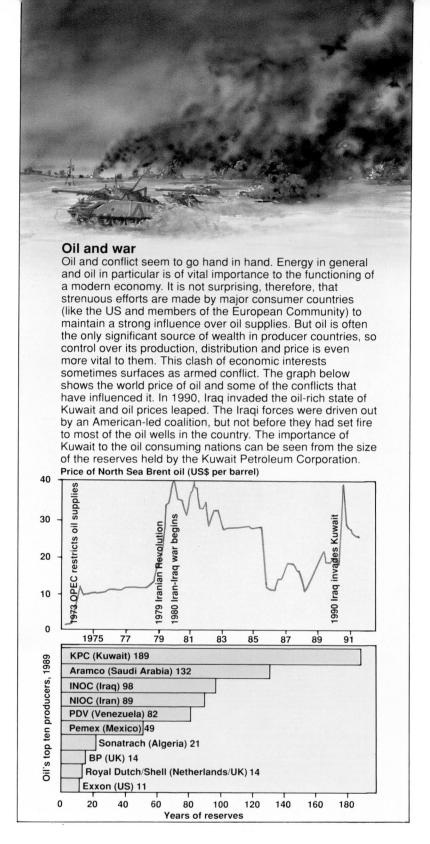

Oil and war

Oil and conflict seem to go hand in hand. Energy in general and oil in particular is of vital importance to the functioning of a modern economy. It is not surprising, therefore, that strenuous efforts are made by major consumer countries (like the US and members of the European Community) to maintain a strong influence over oil supplies. But oil is often the only significant source of wealth in producer countries, so control over its production, distribution and price is even more vital to them. This clash of economic interests sometimes surfaces as armed conflict. The graph below shows the world price of oil and some of the conflicts that have influenced it. In 1990, Iraq invaded the oil-rich state of Kuwait and oil prices leaped. The Iraqi forces were driven out by an American-led coalition, but not before they had set fire to most of the oil wells in the country. The importance of Kuwait to the oil consuming nations can be seen from the size of the reserves held by the Kuwait Petroleum Corporation.

Price of North Sea Brent oil (US$ per barrel)

Graph annotations: 1973 OPEC restricts oil supplies; 1979 Iranian Revolution; 1980 Iran-Iraq war begins; 1990 Iraq invades Kuwait. Years: 1975, 77, 79, 81, 83, 85, 87, 89, 91.

Oil's top ten producers, 1989

- KPC (Kuwait) 189
- Aramco (Saudi Arabia) 132
- INOC (Iraq) 98
- NIOC (Iran) 89
- PDV (Venezuela) 82
- Pemex (Mexico) 49
- Sonatrach (Algeria) 21
- BP (UK) 14
- Royal Dutch/Shell (Netherlands/UK) 14
- Exxon (US) 11

Years of reserves

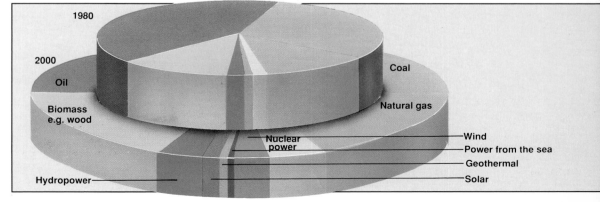

The pie chart shows the way the world's energy use is shared between different sources and how it may have changed by the year 2000.

1980
2000
Oil
Biomass e.g. wood
Hydropower
Coal
Natural gas
Nuclear power
Wind
Power from the sea
Geothermal
Solar

17

7 Manufacturing

Manufacturing is a process which turns raw materials into products using labor, energy and equipment. These products may be 'finished' and ready for sale to consumers (for example, cars) or they may be 'intermediate' and sold to other manufacturers who use them as inputs to production (for example, steel). Both finished and intermediate products may be sold at home or abroad.

Developed countries have a large manufacturing sector, although the share of manufacturing in national output has fallen as the service sector has grown (see SERVICES). As industrialization occurs in developing countries, the pattern of manufacturing around the world changes. Industrializing countries are often able to produce simple goods for lower prices than developed countries because wages are lower (a cost advantage). Developed countries with high wage costs tend to produce more sophisticated products which rely instead on a technological advantage. A third type of advantage is a good supply of raw materials and energy. The success of a manufacturer in international trade depends on its technology and cost advantages relative to its competitors.

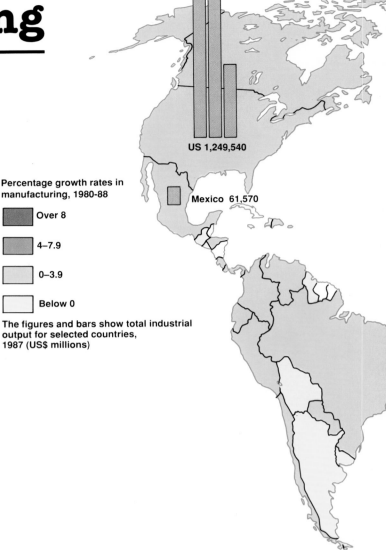

Percentage growth rates in manufacturing, 1980-88

- Over 8
- 4–7.9
- 0–3.9
- Below 0

The figures and bars show total industrial output for selected countries, 1987 (US$ millions)

US 1,249,540

Mexico 61,570

Duisburg is an example of industrial decline in the Ruhr. By 1990, the level of unemployment in Duisburg was twice the German average.

• Duisburg

Industrial dinosaurs

As industrializing countries gain the technology to compete in traditional manufacturing industries, industrial decline often occurs in more developed countries due partly to high wage costs. The manufacturing industries that are hardest hit include iron and steel, ship-building, cars and textiles. Mining sectors are often affected as well. Because the prosperity of the Ruhr in Germany has historically been based on steel and coal, the region has suffered badly from the decline of these traditional industries. Unemployment is higher than the national average and income per capita and economic growth are lower. Between 1985 and 1990, the total number of people in industrial employment in the city of Duisburg fell by 27,000, of which over 10,000 had been employed in the steel and steel engineering industries. Plans to help the Ruhr include the encouragement of small and medium sized businesses, the creation of jobs in modern manufacturing and service sectors, and the installation of modern information and communications systems.

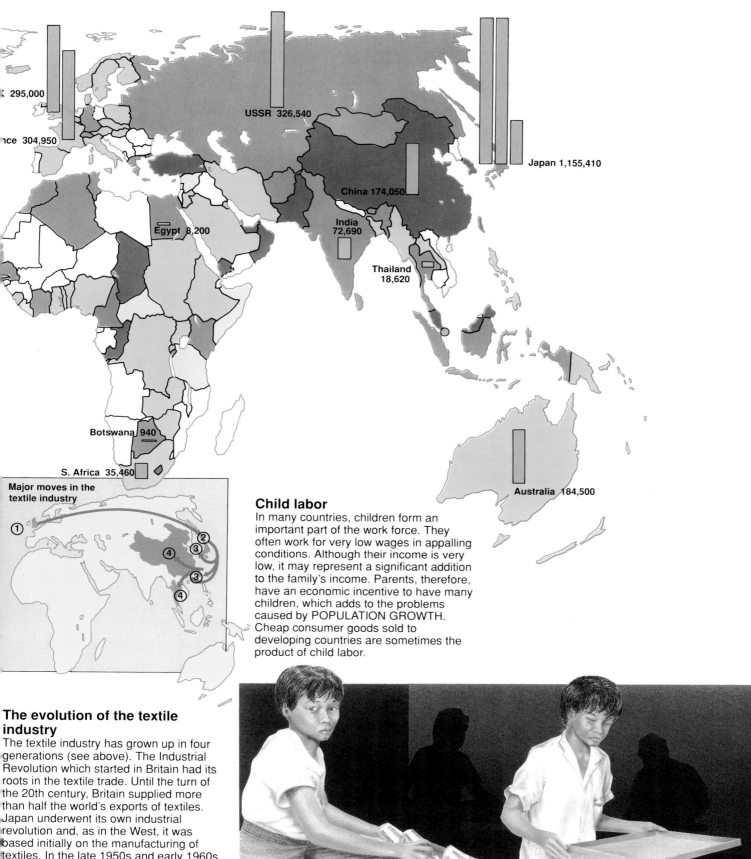

295,000

nce 304,950

USSR 326,540

Japan 1,155,410

China 174,050

Egypt 8,200

India
72,690

Thailand
18,620

Botswana 940

S. Africa 35,460

Australia 184,500

Major moves in the
textile industry

① ② ③ ④ ③ ④

Child labor
In many countries, children form an
important part of the work force. They
often work for very low wages in appalling
conditions. Although their income is very
low, it may represent a significant addition
to the family's income. Parents, therefore,
have an economic incentive to have many
children, which adds to the problems
caused by POPULATION GROWTH.
Cheap consumer goods sold to
developing countries are sometimes the
product of child labor.

The evolution of the textile
industry
The textile industry has grown up in four
generations (see above). The Industrial
Revolution which started in Britain had its
roots in the textile trade. Until the turn of
the 20th century, Britain supplied more
than half the world's exports of textiles.
Japan underwent its own industrial
revolution and, as in the West, it was
based initially on the manufacturing of
textiles. In the late 1950s and early 1960s
a group of Newly Industrializing Countries
(the NICs, including Hong Kong, Taiwan
and South Korea) began to manufacture
textiles. Because wages were low and the
levels of skill and technology required to
produce textiles were also low, these
countries had an advantage. As wage
costs rise in the NICs, the advantage
moves to China and some Southeast
Asian countries, especially Thailand.

8 Services

Unlike agriculture, mining and manufacturing, the products of service industries are not physical goods. For this reason services are sometimes called 'invisibles.' A simple example is a haircut. In return for payment, you do not receive a good, but you do receive a benefit. The same is true of seeing a movie or visiting a doctor. Services is a very broad term which includes many important activities such as banking, insurance, tourism, transportation and communications. Service industries generally play a greater role in developed economies (see DEVELOPMENT). In the industrial countries of the Organization for Economic Cooperation and Development (OECD), they employ more than half the work force and contribute more than half the national product. Due to the decline in traditional manufacturing industries in these countries, services are increasingly important.

Because many services must be consumed at the point where they are produced, service industries contribute relatively less to international trade than manufacturing. Still, trade in services has risen very fast since 1970 and is now worth over US$600 million.

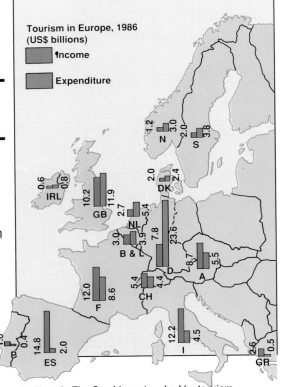

Tourism in Europe, 1986
(US$ billions)
- Income
- Expenditure

Balancing the books

The map shows that the countries of northern Europe spend more on traveling abroad than they earn from visitors. In contrast, tourism is a net earner in the warmer countries of southern Europe. It accounts for about 4% of the national income in Spain, Portugal and Greece.

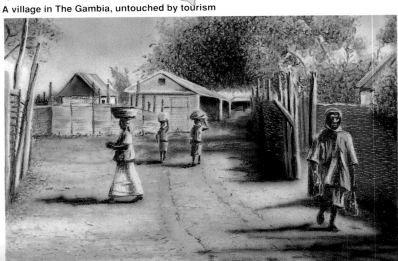

A village in The Gambia, untouched by tourism

British Ports

Services must adapt to technological advances or suffer a decline. The advent of oil supertankers and container ships has meant that ports must provide facilities capable of handling their cargo. Those ports that were unable to do this for physical or financial reasons declined during the 1970s. The west coast ports have all declined, despite the installation of new dock facilities in some, partly because the regions that they serve have been depressed economically and partly because the east coast ports have much closer trading links with the European Community.

Felixstowe +633
Clyde −52 Forth +207
Tyne −18
Tees & Hartlepool +77
Liverpool −19   Hull +5
    King's Lynn
Manchester −49   Harwich +96
Swansea −40   Bristol −35
Cardiff −33   London −9
Plymouth −22   S'hampton +2
   Medway −41
   Dover +519

Major British ports: percentage change in foreign and domestic traffic 1970–1990

The tourist boom

Tourism has become a big business in the last 30 years. Rising incomes in industrial and newly industrializing countries mean that people have more money to spend on vacations. International tourism is now worth nearly $150 billion. This figure does not include cross-border trips which are big money-makers in the countries of Western Europe and the US, Canada and Mexico.

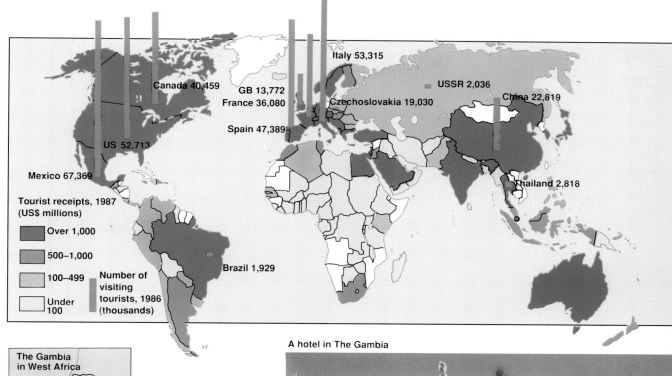

Canada 40,459
US 52,713
Mexico 67,369
Brazil 1,929
Italy 53,315
GB 13,772
France 36,080
Spain 47,389
Czechoslovakia 19,030
USSR 2,036
China 22,819
Thailand 2,818

Tourist receipts, 1987
(US$ millions)

Over 1,000
500–1,000
100–499
Under 100

Number of visiting tourists, 1986 (thousands)

Tourism in The Gambia

Many developing countries are trying to promote tourism in order to earn foreign currency that they can then use to buy the goods they need from other countries. The number of visitors in The Gambia has grown from 20 in 1965 to 114,000 in 1990. Tourism now represents about 10% of the national income and provides Gambians with about

The Gambia in West Africa

7,500 jobs. However, Gambians do not necessarily receive all the benefits of tourism. The better jobs in hotels may be given to people brought in from

overseas, and hotels may prefer to import food and drink rather than support local agriculture. In The Gambia, 60% of the food and 40% of the drink served in hotels is imported. Profits may flow out of the country to foreign owners of the hotels, although the taxes paid on the profits to the Gambian government partly offset this loss.

A hotel in The Gambia

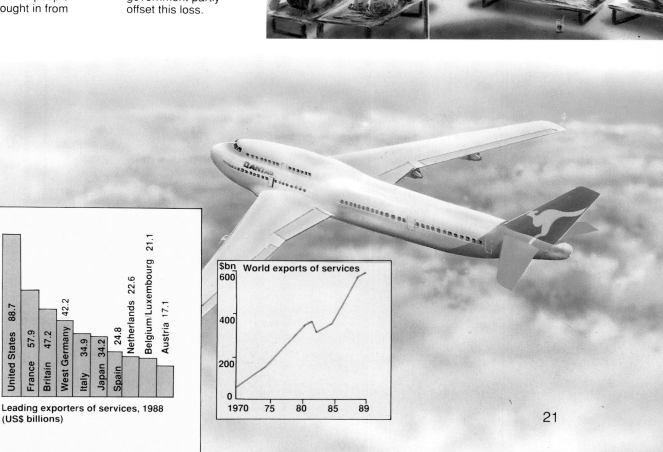

Trade in services

World trade in services is dominated by developed countries because their service sectors are much more established than in developing countries. Also, many exportable services (for example, banking and financial services) are based on quite sophisticated technology, which is more available in developed countries. The US is the largest exporter of services, although as a fraction of national income, exports of services are more important to the economies of many European countries.

United States 88.7
France 57.9
Britain 47.2
West Germany 42.2
Italy 34.9
Japan 34.2
Spain 24.8
Netherlands 22.6
Belgium/Luxembourg 21.1
Austria 17.1

Leading exporters of services, 1988 (US$ billions)

$bn World exports of services
600
400
200
0
1970 75 80 85 89

21

9 Transport & Communications

Transport and communications are vital to economic activity. Passenger transport carries people to such locations as their place of work, while freight transport delivers raw materials, intermediate and finished products. Because transport infrastructure (roads, railways, ports and airports) is very expensive and benefits everyone, governments usually pay for its construction and maintenance out of taxes. Forms of transportation may be public or private. Public transportation is run by the government mostly for passengers. Private transportation includes cars and ships. As a country becomes richer and car ownership increases, the use of public transportation falls.

Communication takes many different forms. Newspapers, television and radio (the mass media) convey information to large numbers of people. Other forms of communication such as the telephone or facsimile machine carry messages from one person to another. Economic transactions usually involve some risks, often because of a lack of information. The communications revolution which has occurred this century means that it is easier to gain the information necessary to make correct decisions quickly. The chance of missing an opportunity is also lower and this boosts the level of activity in an economy.

Communications Revolution

Rapid developments in technology have reduced the cost and increased the value of communication. In 1983 it cost around $13,000 a month to lease the US half of a private transatlantic voice channel for telephone calls, but now the cost is only about $5,000. The cost of processing information on computers has also fallen – to half its 1975 level.

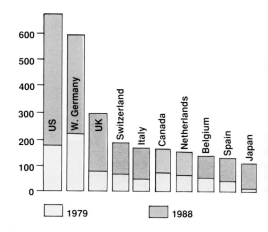

Outgoing international calls in selected countries (millions)

Countries (left to right): US, W. Germany, UK, Switzerland, Italy, Canada, Netherlands, Belgium, Spain, Japan

☐ 1979   ▨ 1988

The Channel tunnel

In 1986 the decision to build a tunnel under the Channel between Britain and France was announced. It has been the largest and most expensive construction project ever undertaken in Western Europe. Trains will run through the tunnel carrying passengers, cars, trucks and freight. The tunnel was necessary to improve links between Britain and the rest of Europe, offering an alternative to sea and air transport. Freight trains will be able to run all the way between Britain and mainland Europe without the interruption of the unloading and loading involved in sea crossings.

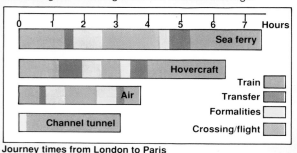

Sea ferry

Hovercraft

Air

Channel tunnel

Train
Transfer
Formalities
Crossing/flight

Journey times from London to Paris

**Road density
(miles/square
mile)**

■ Over 1.2
▨ 0.9–1.2
▨ 0.6–0.9
▨ 0.3–0.6
▨ 0.06–0.3
□ Below 0.06

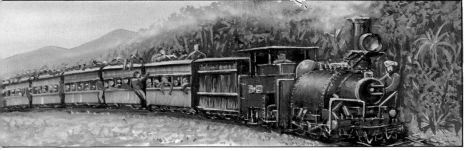

Indian rail
India has the fourth largest railway network in the world, after the USSR, US and Canada. Although the network is quite comprehensive, most of the rolling stock and tracks are old, and the system is inefficient. One of the problems facing India, is energy supplies. Although coal is available, deficiencies in the transport system, especially the railways, make the delivery of coal to places where it is needed very difficult.

Road pricing in Hong Kong
Many cities suffer from peak rush hours when the roads become very congested with cars carrying people to and from work. The costs caused by the delays and air pollution are a source of great concern. Many measures have been suggested to ease the problem. One idea that has been tested in Hong Kong is a road pricing system which charges road users according to the route and the time of day (see below). Driving a car in the central business district in peak hour attracts the highest charge. Such a scheme can be used to promote the use of public transportation, by making buses exempt.

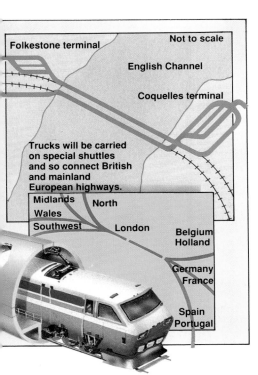

Not to scale

Folkestone terminal

English Channel

Coquelles terminal

Trucks will be carried on special shuttles and so connect British and mainland European highways.

Midlands North
Wales
Southwest   London
                  Belgium
                  Holland

                  Germany
                  France

                  Spain
                  Portugal

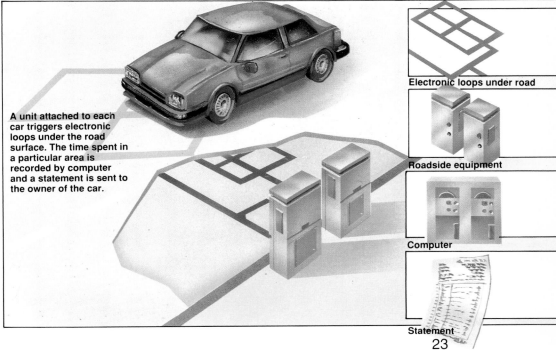

A unit attached to each car triggers electronic loops under the road surface. The time spent in a particular area is recorded by computer and a statement is sent to the owner of the car.

Electronic loops under road

Roadside equipment

Computer

Statement

23

10 Households

The last six topics have all been about different economic sectors, or, to put it another way, different kinds of economic activity. They have focused on the 'what' and 'how' questions introduced in AN IMAGINARY ECONOMY: 'what should the economy produce and how should the economy produce it?.' This spread and the next three look at 'who' is involved in the economy – the players on the economic stage – and at 'who gets what out of it and who puts what in?.' Between them, these economic agents shape the answers to the what, how, and who questions in every society.

The household is the basic unit of economic organization. All households consume goods and services and most supply labor. Some also have savings on which they can earn interest. A few own shares which give them a share of company profits (see MONEY AND ASSETS). Most households, though, get the bulk of their income from LABOR. Here, we are concerned mainly with the way households use their income and focus on consumption.

Figure gives total consumer spending per capita (US$)

US $12,233

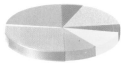

Japan $11,126

Czechoslovakia $5,088

Tunisia $923

Senegal $404

Average consumer spending on:

- Food/drink
- Clothing
- Energy/housing
- Household goods
- Health
- Transport/communications
- Leisure/other

Informal housing

Next to food and water, the most important thing a household needs is shelter. Shelter comes in many different forms but there is a simple distinction that is often made between formal and informal housing. Nearly all housing in countries like the UK and US is formal but many people in the Third World live in informal or squatter settlements. A squatter settlement is one in which the land is not owned by the residents, instead they have simply taken it over or begun to live on it.

Expenditure distribution

The poorer the country, the greater the share of total spending that goes on food and drink. The wealthier the country, the greater the share that goes on leisure.

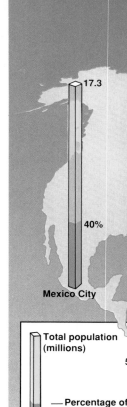

Mexico City

17.3

40%

Total population (millions)

5

— Percentage of population in informal hous

= 1 million peo
Selected major cities (figures give percentage of populati in informal housing)

Self-built housing in Ken

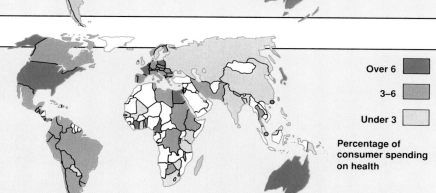

Over 5,000

1,000–5,000

Under 1,000

Total consumer spending per capita (US$)

Over 6

3–6

Under 3

Percentage of consumer spending on health

Spending on health

The maps show that some countries with very high percentages of spending on health also have very high total spending per capita, such as the US, but not all of them. In those countries where most health care is provided free to users, such as the UK, the percentage of household expenditure devoted to health is very small. In the end, of course, health services in these countries have to be paid for through taxes.

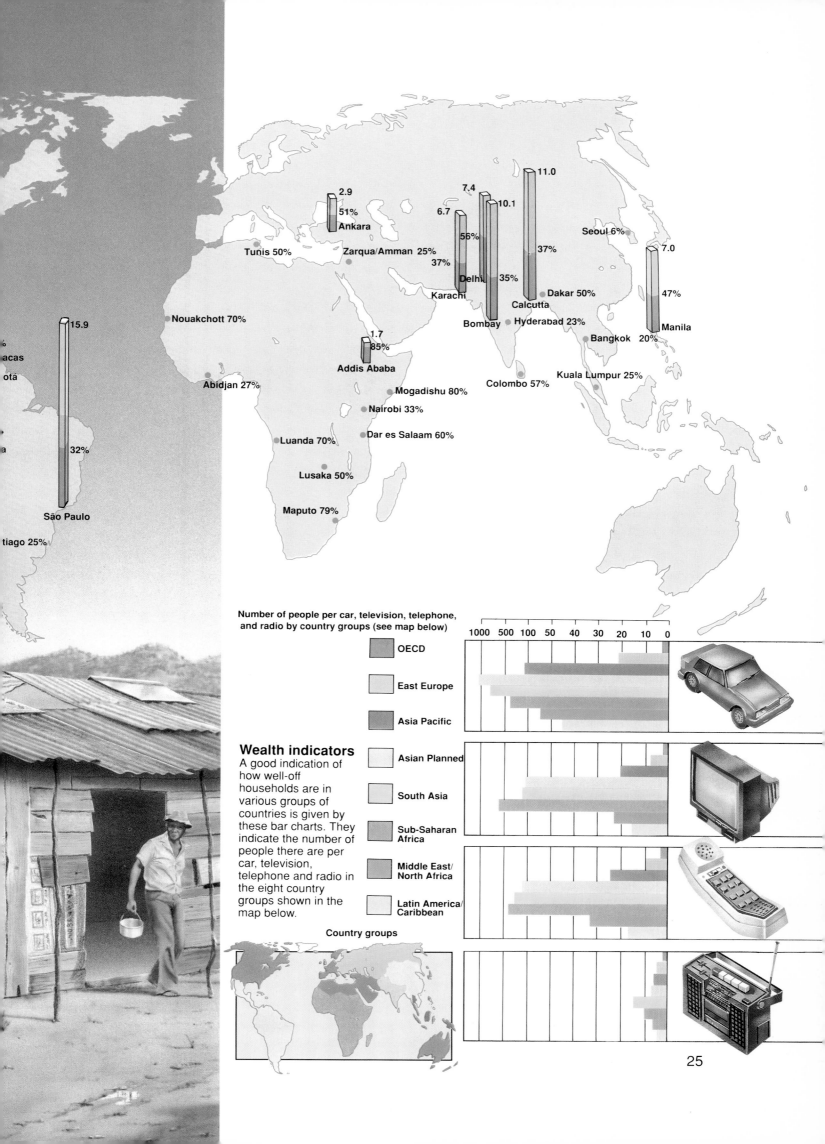

2.9
51%
Ankara

Tunis 50%

Zarqua/Amman 25%

7.4
56%
Delhi

6.7
37%
Karachi

10.1
35%
Bombay

11.0
37%
Calcutta

Seoul 6%

7.0
47%
Manila

20%

Dakar 50%

Hyderabad 23%

Bangkok

Kuala Lumpur 25%

Colombo 57%

Nouakchott 70%

1.7
85%
Addis Ababa

Abidjan 27%

Mogadishu 80%

Nairobi 33%

Dar es Salaam 60%

Luanda 70%

Lusaka 50%

Maputo 79%

15.9
32%
São Paulo

acas

otá

a

tiago 25%

Number of people per car, television, telephone, and radio by country groups (see map below)

1000 500 100 50 40 30 20 10 0

OECD

East Europe

Asia Pacific

Asian Planned

South Asia

Sub-Saharan Africa

Middle East/ North Africa

Latin America/ Caribbean

Country groups

Wealth indicators

A good indication of how well-off households are in various groups of countries is given by these bar charts. They indicate the number of people there are per car, television, telephone and radio in the eight country groups shown in the map below.

25

11 Labor

The work force includes everyone who is working or looking for work (see UNEMPLOYMENT). People who are working may be employed, self-employed or unpaid workers in a family business. As countries become more developed, the work force tends to move from agriculture to industry, and then from industry to services (see DEVELOPMENT).

The amount of production per capita depends on the 'participation rate' – the number of people of working age (15-64) who are in the work force. The map (top right) shows participation rates around the world. The higher the participation rate, the higher the ratio of workers to non-workers in an economy. One important factor influencing the participation rate is the number of women in the work force. This is high in Scandinavian countries where child care and maternity leave arrangements are very advanced. It is also high in some African countries where women traditionally do most of the work on the land. Another factor which influences the amount of production in an economy is the amount of time that people spend at work, which tends to get shorter as countries become richer. This is largely because 'productivity' or output per worker increases where there is better equipment available for the work force to use, and it is far superior in developed countries because businesses have greater resources to invest in good equipment.

Searching for work
Large numbers of people travel to other countries to find work. Because the waiting period to migrate legally can be very long, many workers resort to illegal entry by avoiding border controls. For example, one million Mexicans are thought to enter the US each year, crossing the Rio Grande. Although they often take the worst and lowest paid jobs in the US, the wages they earn are still much higher than in Mexico.

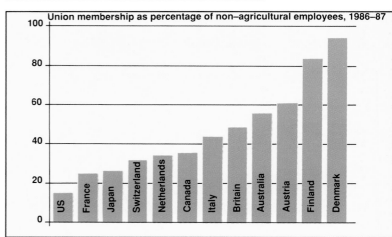

Union membership as percentage of non–agricultural employees, 1986–87

(bar chart, left to right: US, France, Japan, Switzerland, Netherlands, Canada, Italy, Britain, Australia, Austria, Finland, Denmark)

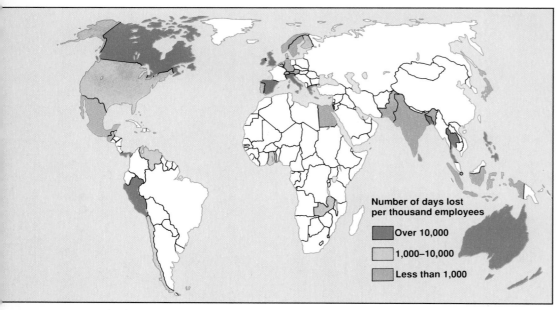

Number of days lost per thousand employees

- Over 10,000
- 1,000–10,000
- Less than 1,000

Workers unite
During the Industrial Revolution, wages and conditions were very poor, so employee organizations called 'trade unions' were formed to try to improve the lot of their members. Throughout history, trade unions have been vital to the interests of employees and still play an important role. The outcome of wage negotiations is crucial to economic performance. If wages are set too high, then it is very hard for businesses to produce goods at a competitive price. If wages are set too low, then the workers' standard of living is unnecessarily lowered. During negotiations, conflict can arise between employers and trade unions, and trade unions may 'go on strike' and refuse to work. Generally, unions are strongest in the traditional manufacturing industries where workers tend to be concentrated in very large factories, making the organization of unions easier.

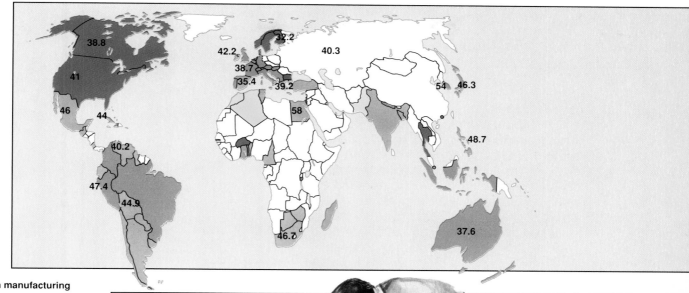

Size of work force as percentage of population (participation rate)

- 50 and over
- 40–49
- 30–39
- Less than 30

Figures give the numbers of hours worked per week in manufacturing

The informal economy in Peru

Like many developing countries, Peru has experienced an enormous migration of people from depressed rural areas to the cities, especially the capital, Lima. A very large number of its labor force work in small businesses which operate outside the legal system. As a result they do not pay taxes, but they also have no security such as the right to keep their property. For example, there are many *ambulantes* or street vendors who offer a range of goods in competition with large retail outlets. The informal sector is important to the economies of many developing countries. For this reason international aid agencies have begun to concentrate on helping small businesses in the informal sector as a way of creating more jobs.

Industrial relations and productivity in Japan

Industrial relations are the relations between employer and employee. They are very important to the productivity of business because satisfied and motivated employees are likely to work harder. Japan has enjoyed very high productivity growth since World War II. Part of the reason may be its unique industrial relations system, which rests on three pillars: *shushin koyo* system which guarantees long-term employment; *nenko joretsu* system under which earnings grow the longer the employee stays; and enterprise unions within each firm which contain employees of different skills and ranks. The first two pillars mean that workers are less likely to leave their jobs in Japan. In return, companies keep the work force employed even during difficult times. It is not unusual for Japanese companies to organize exercise classes for the work force, and the working day may start with a pep session reinforcing the company's goals. While the Japanese system has improved the productivity of the work force, some would argue that the rigid lifestyle imposed on workers is not socially desirable.

About 60% of the work force in Peru is employed in the informal economy, producing around one third of the country's national product.

27

12 Business

In an economy, businesses are the basic units responsible for organizing production. They produce goods and services for sale to households, the government and other businesses. The aim of businesses is to make a profit. To do this, the revenue they earn from sales must be more than the costs of production. The major costs facing businesses can be divided into fixed and running costs. Fixed costs (also called overhead), such as the cost of building a factory and installing equipment, do not depend closely on the amount of goods produced. The cost will remain the same whether the factory operates for two or twenty hours each day. In contrast, running costs, including wages, raw materials and energy, depend on the quantity of goods produced.

Businesses come in many different sizes, ranging from single traders to huge multinational corporations (see FOREIGN INVESTMENT). The map shows that the largest corporations in the world are based in industrialized countries, although they operate worldwide. These corporations earn more from sales than the national income of many developing countries.

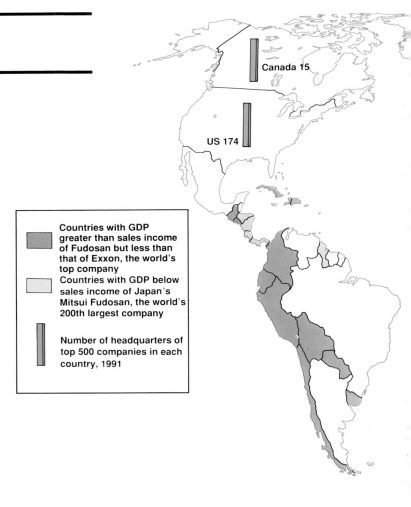

Canada 15

US 174

Countries with GDP greater than sales income of Fudosan but less than that of Exxon, the world's top company

Countries with GDP below sales income of Japan's Mitsui Fudosan, the world's 200th largest company

Number of headquarters of top 500 companies in each country, 1991

A business may begin with work at home

Growth may involve the opening of a small shop

Life cycles

Individual products, and sometimes the businesses that make them, follow a life cycle of development. Often, a business is based on new technology which results in better products. Early growth may be slow, due to the need to set up a production process and sales and distribution channels. If demand for the product increases, the business expands rapidly. As it reaches maturity, sales continue to grow, but at a slower rate. To reduce costs and promote sales, businesses may establish subsidiary companies in other countries. Usually, businesses in the mature phase face strong competition from other businesses, and the demand for particular products may decline as superior substitutes appear. A business can remain profitable by developing new products to sell.

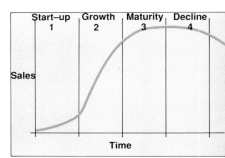

Stages in the life of a business

As a business matures it may open its own factory

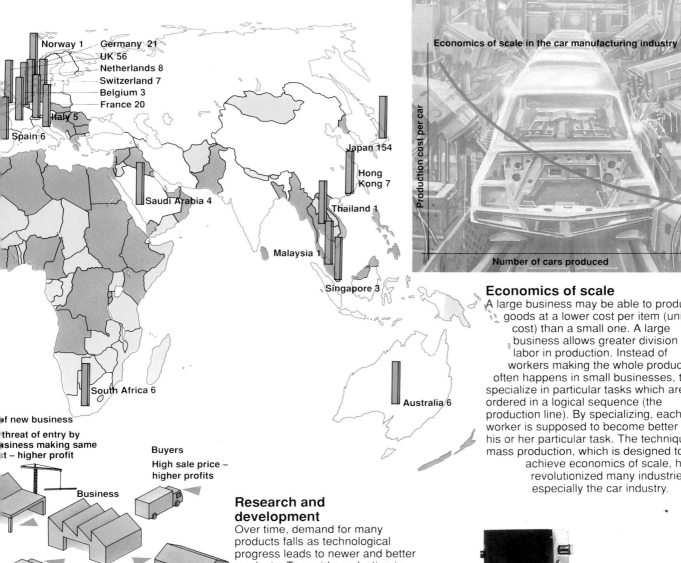

Norway 1
Germany 21
UK 56
Netherlands 8
Switzerland 7
Belgium 3
France 20
Italy 5
Spain 6
Saudi Arabia 4
Japan 154
Hong Kong 7
Thailand 1
Malaysia 1
Singapore 3
South Africa 6
Australia 6

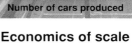

Economics of scale in the car manufacturing industry

Production cost per car

Number of cars produced

Economics of scale

A large business may be able to produce goods at a lower cost per item (unit cost) than a small one. A large business allows greater division of labor in production. Instead of workers making the whole product, as often happens in small businesses, they specialize in particular tasks which are ordered in a logical sequence (the production line). By specializing, each worker is supposed to become better at his or her particular task. The technique of mass production, which is designed to achieve economics of scale, has revolutionized many industries, especially the car industry.

f new business

threat of entry by
usiness making same
t – higher profit

Buyers
High sale price –
higher profits

Business

Substitutes

ice – higher profits
Lower threat by substitute
products – higher profits

Business strategy

Businesses try to keep their costs as low as possible, while earning the highest revenue from sales. They must be profitable in order to continue operating. Except where a business has a monopoly, it faces competition from other businesses trying to sell similar goods and services. It needs, therefore, to maintain or increase its share of total sales or its profit margin on each product sold.

There are two basic sources of competitive advantage: lower price and higher quality. Lower price means that buyers are more likely to prefer a firm's product to its competitor's, provided the quality is similar, and so total sales will be high. Better quality means that buyers may be prepared to pay a higher mark-up (the difference between production cost and sale price), which would lead to higher profit margins. Higher quality is often associated with a well-known brand name, obtained through careful attention to quality, backed by skillful advertising and marketing.

Research and development

Over time, demand for many products falls as technological progress leads to newer and better products. To avoid a reduction in sales, a business must have access to new technology. One way of doing this is to spend money on discovering new ideas for products (research) and turning these ideas into commercial products (development). Businesses that can maintain a technological edge over their competitors usually earn higher profits. Research and development (R & D) spending often takes time to yield benefits. Because they want to make short-term profits, many businesses are reluctant to spend adequately on R & D, although it is important for the competitiveness of businesses and national economics in the long run.

Research and development expenditure as percentage of sales

	UK	US	Germany	Japan

(%) 0–5 scale

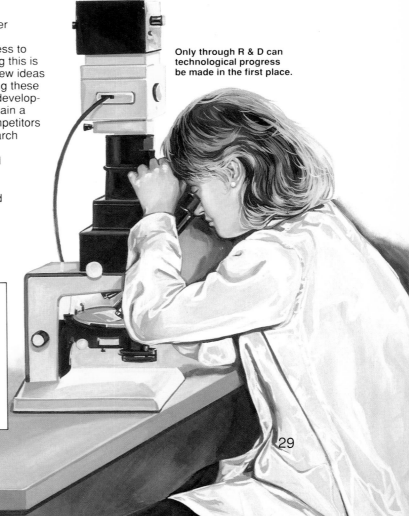

Only through R & D can technological progress be made in the first place.

13 Government

Governments play an essential role in economies. They influence all the major economic activities in society, including production, consumption and investment, both directly and indirectly. One of the direct ways is by producing goods and services. All governments directly provide defense and transport infrastructure and some produce agricultural and industrial goods themselves. Another direct way in which governments affect economies is by spending, which has a huge impact as the government is the largest consumer in the economy. Equally important is the way that governments influence economies indirectly by using policy tools. The most important tools used by governments to manage economies are taxation and interest rates. Governments also affect economic activity by making regulations covering a wide range of activities, some of which try to insure that competition between businesses is fair. Economies where governments directly control most activity, such as China, are called *centrally planned*. Production throughout the economy is set by long-term plans made by the government. In contrast, in *free market* economies such as the US countries, governments tend to manage the economy indirectly. However, there is no such thing as a completely free market economy, and therefore industrial economies are referred to as *mixed*, with some parts controlled by the government and others left to free market forces.

The welfare state

Governments spend a great deal of money in providing health care, education, housing and social security. The aim is to guarantee a minimum standard of living to the whole population. Unfortunately, developing countries do not always have the resources to achieve this aim. Even in developed countries, homelessness and the over-crowding of hospitals are of great concern.

Taxation

Taxation is a compulsory transfer of money from individuals or businesses to the government. It is by far the biggest source of government revenue in most countries. There are two basic types of taxation: direct and indirect (see below). Personal income tax accounts for a smaller share of government revenue in developing countries because the operation of a system to tax individuals is expensive. Developing countries rely much more on trade taxation (customs duties). Taxation involves social as well as economic goals because the money raised by the government is used to provide welfare services. Also, personal income tax is often levied at a higher rate on higher incomes, which helps to redistribute money from the rich to the poor.

Government spending

Education is a major item of government expenditure for both developed and developing countries, but the fraction spent on health, housing and social security grows as countries become richer. Generally, the proportion of government spending on investment projects is far higher in developing countries, where the private sector is less able to raise the funds itself.

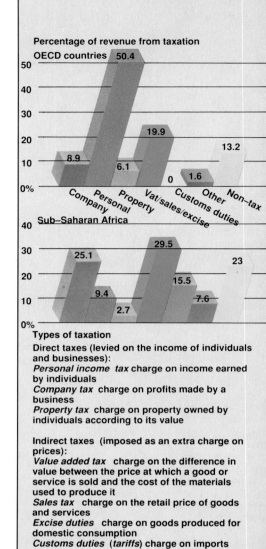

Percentage of revenue from taxation

OECD countries: Company 8.9, Personal 50.4, Property 6.1, Vat/sales/excise 19.9, Customs duties 0, Other 1.6, Non-tax 13.2

Sub-Saharan Africa: Company 25.1, Personal 9.4, Property 2.7, Vat/sales/excise 29.5, Customs duties 15.5, Other 7.6, Non-tax 23

Types of taxation

Direct taxes (levied on the income of individuals and businesses):
Personal income tax charge on income earned by individuals
Company tax charge on profits made by a business
Property tax charge on property owned by individuals according to its value

Indirect taxes (imposed as an extra charge on prices):
Value added tax charge on the difference in value between the price at which a good or service is sold and the cost of the materials used to produce it
Sales tax charge on the retail price of goods and services
Excise duties charge on goods produced for domestic consumption
Customs duties (*tariffs*) charge on imports

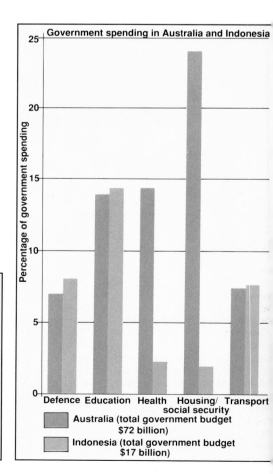

Government spending in Australia and Indonesia

(vertical axis: Percentage of government spending)
Categories: Defence, Education, Health, Housing/social security, Transport

Australia (total government budget $72 billion)
Indonesia (total government budget $17 billion)

Defense	Housing/social security	Education	Health
1 UAE 45.3	1 Sweden 54.4	1 Pakistan 29.5	1 Iceland 22.8
2 Syria 40.4	2 Luxembourg 51.9	2 Ghana 25.7	2 Costa Rica 19.3
3 Oman 38.2	3 Uruguay 49.5	3 Ecuador 25.1	3 France 19.1
4 North Yemen 31.2	4 Austria 47.5	4 Fiji 20.7	4 Yugoslavia 16.6
5 Israel 27.2	5 Malta 44.6	5 Côte d'Ivoire 20.5	5 Panama 16.4
6 Jordan 26.5	6 Belgium 43.2	6 Togo 19.9	6 West Germany 15.8
7 Uganda 26.3	7 West Germany 42.6	7 Colombia 19.7	7 Switzerland 15.7
8 El Salvador 25.7	8 Spain 40.7	8 Venezuela 19.6	8 Australia 14.4
9 Peru 20.0	9 Denmark 40.4	9 Iran 19.6	9 Bahamas 13.5
10 Egypt 19.5	10 France 40.3	10 Thailand 19.3	10 Canada 13.3

Top ten spenders, 1988 (percentage of total government spending)

Guns or butter?

Military spending has absorbed about 5% of the world's resources over the past 20 years. This has meant that fewer resources have been available for social expenditures on health, education and social security, as well as economic development projects financed by the government. In addition, because governments need to raise taxes to cover defense spending, businesses and households have less money for consumption and investment, and so contribute less to economic growth. The costs of high defense spending are more severe in developing countries where resources are very scarce. Yet the fraction of Gross Domestic Product (GDP) devoted to military expenditure is higher than in industrial countries.

The reunification of Germany

On October 2, 1990 the formal reunification of East and West Germany occurred. Prior to reunification, East Germany had a centrally planned economy, but it has now adopted the economic system of West Germany. Serious problems have emerged (see the graph below, right). Almost twice as much energy is consumed by east German factories as by west German factories to produce goods of the same value. Environmental problems are also very serious in the east.

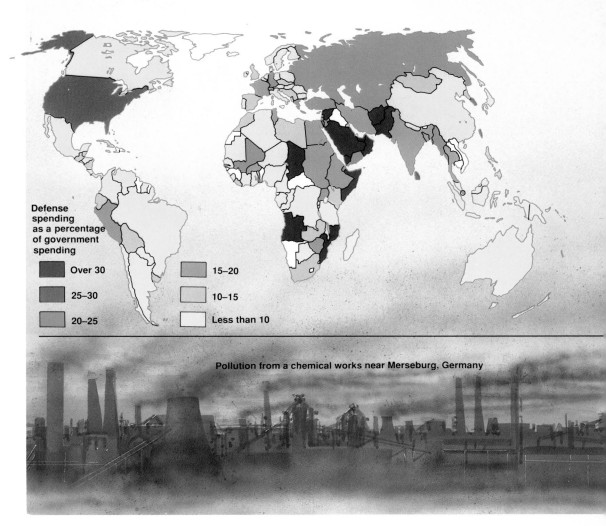

Defense spending as a percentage of government spending

- Over 30
- 25–30
- 20–25
- 15–20
- 10–15
- Less than 10

Pollution from a chemical works near Merseburg, Germany

Changing economies

Recently, as a result of dramatic political events, the countries of Eastern Europe have begun to shift from centrally planned to free market economies. In October 1989 Poland decided to 'cross the chasm in one leap' with a series of rapid reforms. In contrast, Hungary has followed a much more gradual path. The successful transition to free market economies will depend on foreign investment, and to help the process a new international bank has been set up: the European Bank for Reconstruction and Development. It will encourage the transition to free market economies and promote private enterprise.

Budget deficits

In most countries, government spending has grown very fast. Often, revenue has grown more slowly so governments are spending more than they raise from taxes, resulting in budget deficits. Governments have to then borrow money to cover the shortfall. The map above shows that most governments fail to balance their budgets. A large budget deficit may indicate that a government is not doing a good job of managing the economy. In Brazil and Argentina a poor system of tax collection, spending to prop up inefficient state-owned industry and a large bureaucracy have resulted in enormous deficits. These deficits have contributed to hyperinflation and foreign debt. Budget deficits, however, may be useful if the money, which is borrowed to bridge the gap between government revenue and spending, is used for investment in projects which will provide enough income in the future to repay the loan, and make a profit.

Budget surpluses and deficits
- Surplus
- Deficit

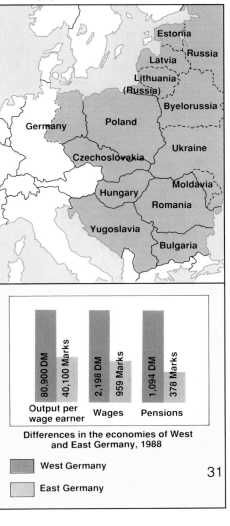

The changing face of Eastern Europe

Estonia, Russia, Latvia, Lithuania (Russia), Byelorussia, Germany, Poland, Ukraine, Czechoslovakia, Moldavia, Hungary, Romania, Yugoslavia, Bulgaria

	Output per wage earner	Wages	Pensions
West Germany	80,900 DM	2,198 DM	1,094 DM
East Germany	40,100 Marks	959 Marks	378 Marks

Differences in the economies of West and East Germany, 1988

- West Germany
- East Germany

14 Income Inequality

One of the major problems in world economics is the vast gulf in the standards of living between different countries. People who live in the rich industrial countries have an average annual income of about $17,000 each. People who live in the countries of Sub-Saharan Africa and south Asia have an annual income of about $350 each. In the poorest countries of these regions, incomes may be lower than $150 per person.

The usual measure of the standard of living is national income per capita (the *average* income). This measure may be misleading because it does not give any information about the way wealth is distributed within each country. It may also be misleading because the cost of living varies among countries, so that $100 will buy more goods and services in one country than another. Whatever measure is used, the overall picture is bleak for the majority of the world's population and solving this problem is the greatest challenge facing the world today.

Income within individual countries

The average income of a country does not give any idea of who receives the lion's share of national income and who receives very little. This is important to know because it tells us just how badly off the poorest people in society are. The examples selected (see below) are typical of low, middle and high income countries. The top and bottom parts of the bars show the percentages of national income that go respectively to the wealthiest 20% and poorest 20% of the population.

People lining up in Poland to purchase goods

Cost of living

Goods and services in some countries may be cheaper or more expensive than in other countries. As a result, the purchasing power of a person's income will vary from country to country. This variation in what is called the cost of living can have a dramatic effect on the standard of living. After adjustment for purchasing power, the US turns out to have the highest income per capita in the world. In Japan, although the average income per capita is considerably higher than in the US, the high cost of living means that the standard of living is reduced to 71% of the US level. The adjustment goes the other way for both Singapore and Sri Lanka, due to their lower cost of living. Singapore overtakes Japan, although its national income per capita is less than 40% of Japan's.

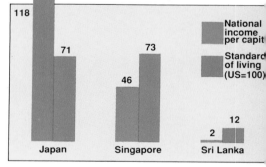

Incomes and living standards compared to the US

Legend:
- National income per capita
- Standard of living (US=100)

Japan: 118, 71
Singapore: 46, 73
Sri Lanka: 2, 12

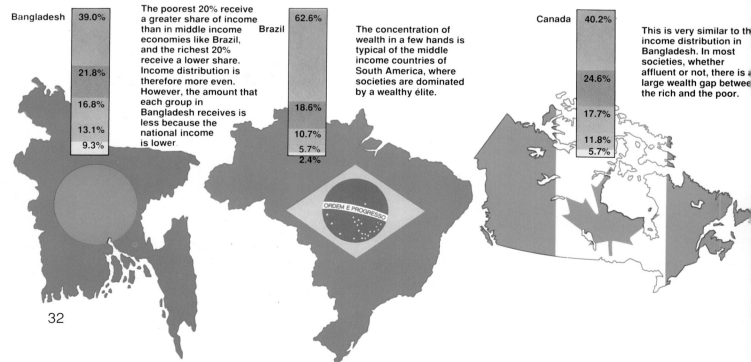

Bangladesh
39.0%
21.8%
16.8%
13.1%
9.3%

The poorest 20% receive a greater share of income than in middle income economies like Brazil, and the richest 20% receive a lower share. Income distribution is therefore more even. However, the amount that each group in Bangladesh receives is less because the national income is lower.

Brazil
62.6%
18.6%
10.7%
5.7%
2.4%

The concentration of wealth in a few hands is typical of the middle income countries of South America, where societies are dominated by a wealthy élite.

Canada
40.2%
24.6%
17.7%
11.8%
5.7%

This is very similar to the income distribution in Bangladesh. In most societies, whether affluent or not, there is a large wealth gap between the rich and the poor.

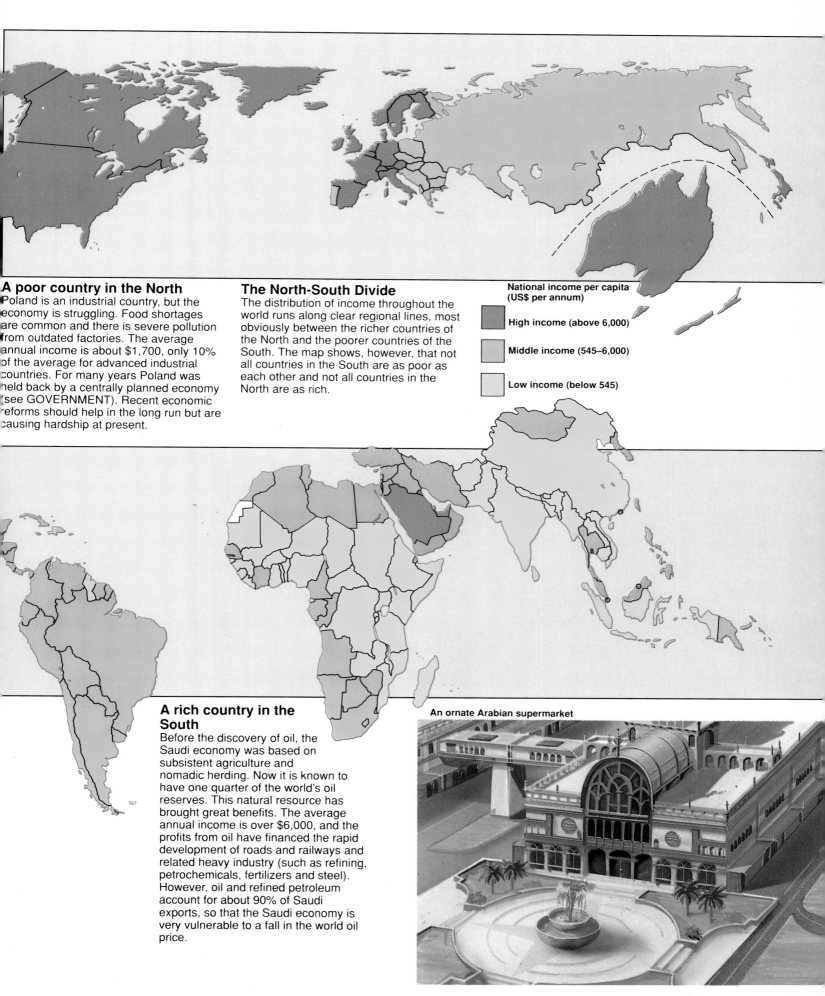

A poor country in the North

Poland is an industrial country, but the economy is struggling. Food shortages are common and there is severe pollution from outdated factories. The average annual income is about $1,700, only 10% of the average for advanced industrial countries. For many years Poland was held back by a centrally planned economy (see GOVERNMENT). Recent economic reforms should help in the long run but are causing hardship at present.

The North-South Divide

The distribution of income throughout the world runs along clear regional lines, most obviously between the richer countries of the North and the poorer countries of the South. The map shows, however, that not all countries in the South are as poor as each other and not all countries in the North are as rich.

National income per capita (US$ per annum)

High income (above 6,000)

Middle income (545–6,000)

Low income (below 545)

A rich country in the South

Before the discovery of oil, the Saudi economy was based on subsistent agriculture and nomadic herding. Now it is known to have one quarter of the world's oil reserves. This natural resource has brought great benefits. The average annual income is over $6,000, and the profits from oil have financed the rapid development of roads and railways and related heavy industry (such as refining, petrochemicals, fertilizers and steel). However, oil and refined petroleum account for about 90% of Saudi exports, so that the Saudi economy is very vulnerable to a fall in the world oil price.

An ornate Arabian supermarket

15 Poverty and Hunger

There are more than 1,000 million people in the world who are chronically hungry and every year 13–18 million people die as a result of hunger. Twenty-four people die from hunger and hunger-related diseases every minute of every day and 18 of them are children under the age of five. Thus, to see where hunger strikes, we can map the distribution of infant mortality rates. This does not tell us precisely what the pattern of hunger is but it gives us a clear indication.

Types of hunger

Chronic malnutrition is the most widespread. It occurs when, over a long period of time, an individual consumes less calories and protein than their body requires.

Malnutrition occurs when there is a major shortage, or excess, of specific nutrients. A quarter of a million children become blind every year as a result of vitamin A deficiency.

Malabsorbative hunger results from the body's inability to absorb nutrients from food due to intestinal parasites and severe protein deficiency.

Seasonal hunger is associated with the agricultural cycle. It tends to occur annually when the previous year's food runs out before the next year's can be harvested.

Famine is a widespread failure of people to gain access to food. It sometimes results from a general decline in the availability of food in a region but it can have other causes (see right).

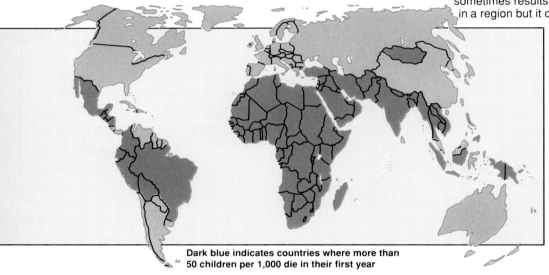

Dark blue indicates countries where more than 50 children per 1,000 die in their first year

Average calorie supplies

To be fit and healthy, the human body needs calories, protein, vitamins and other nutrients. According to the United Nations, the average person needs at least 2,400 calories every day. The map below shows countries where average calorie supplies are below the required level. Remember, however, that averages disguise variations; some people in these countries are fairly well fed but many others suffer from chronic malnutrition (see INCOME INEQUALITY).

The hunger cycle

0–6 months: receives protection from breast milk, but mothers may be undernourished

6 months–2 years: pov... can mean inadequate solid foods unhygienic living environmen...

Adult: poor diet and large work-load for pregnant mothers; one in six babies born underweight

3 years: lis... child does... demand the stimulation... necessary... developme...

Teenager–adult: poorly paid job, lack of strength and inadequate diet

6 years: lack of energy means poor performance at school

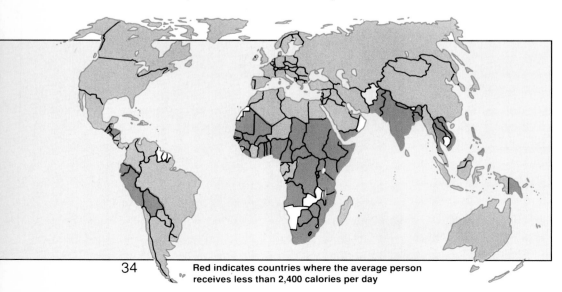

Red indicates countries where the average person receives less than 2,400 calories per day

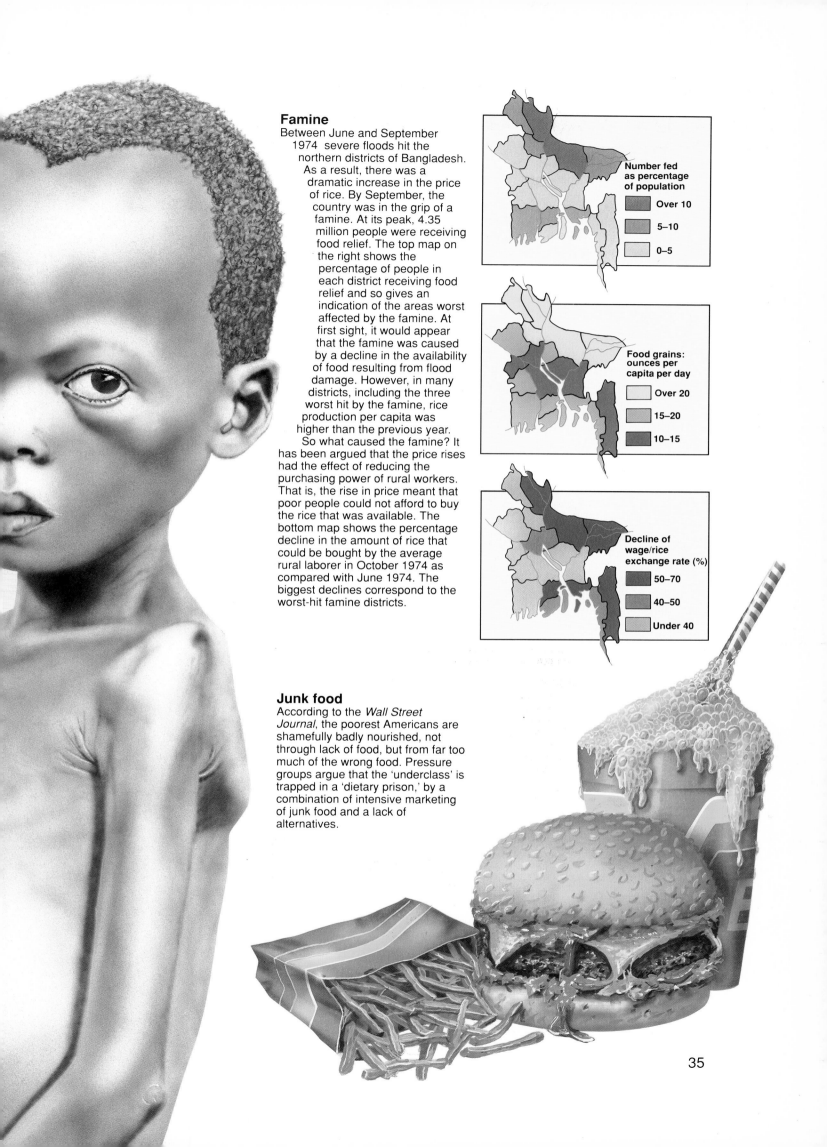

Famine

Between June and September 1974 severe floods hit the northern districts of Bangladesh. As a result, there was a dramatic increase in the price of rice. By September, the country was in the grip of a famine. At its peak, 4.35 million people were receiving food relief. The top map on the right shows the percentage of people in each district receiving food relief and so gives an indication of the areas worst affected by the famine. At first sight, it would appear that the famine was caused by a decline in the availability of food resulting from flood damage. However, in many districts, including the three worst hit by the famine, rice production per capita was higher than the previous year.

So what caused the famine? It has been argued that the price rises had the effect of reducing the purchasing power of rural workers. That is, the rise in price meant that poor people could not afford to buy the rice that was available. The bottom map shows the percentage decline in the amount of rice that could be bought by the average rural laborer in October 1974 as compared with June 1974. The biggest declines correspond to the worst-hit famine districts.

Number fed as percentage of population
- Over 10
- 5–10
- 0–5

Food grains: ounces per capita per day
- Over 20
- 15–20
- 10–15

Decline of wage/rice exchange rate (%)
- 50–70
- 40–50
- Under 40

Junk food

According to the *Wall Street Journal*, the poorest Americans are shamefully badly nourished, not through lack of food, but from far too much of the wrong food. Pressure groups argue that the 'underclass' is trapped in a 'dietary prison,' by a combination of intensive marketing of junk food and a lack of alternatives.

35

16 Population Growth

In 1990 the population of the world was nearly 5.5 billion, more than twice its size in 1950. The number of people is expected to reach 6.25 billion by the turn of the century and 8.5 billion by 2025. How long the globe can cope with such increasing numbers is a pressing issue for world debate.

There are two main views as to what might happen in the future. One is that population growth at the present rate will lead to disaster because the world has only fixed amounts of land and resources that will eventually run out. The other is that technology will come to the rescue and allow the Earth to support increasing numbers of people (see AGRICULTURE). The truth probably lies somewhere between these extreme views. The present rate of population growth is not sustainable forever. Some essential resources may run out before alternatives are discovered, and the damage to the environment may be severe (see ENVIRONMENT). Technological advances will certainly be made, but may only be enough to keep living standards from falling.

Is population growth good or bad news?

Optimists believe that more people will speed up technological progress by increasing the value of new technology. For example, the ability to build an apartment block may not be much use to a small community on a desert island, but is important in densely populated centers. In 1972 a pessimistic view was taken by a report called *The Limits to Growth*. It predicted that within 80 years the world would face disaster due to a shortage of resources. Fixed resources, such as energy, would simply run out, while renewable resources, such as land, would be damaged by overuse.

China

To slow down the growth rate of China's population a rule was introduced in 1984 restricting each couple to one child. This has reduced the birth rate in cities but has not been successful in rural areas, where the value of an extra person to work the land is worth more to parents than the fine for having more than one child. The policy also conflicted with another government policy to reward farmers for increased production.

Malaysia

The Malaysian government announced a plan in 1985 to increase the size of Malaysia's population from 15 million to 80 million. The idea was that with a larger number of consumers, Malaysian industries would be able to take advantage of economies of scale (see BUSINESS) to establish a solid base in Malaysia. From this base they would be in a better position to compete in world trade. The policy seems to have had little effect on the birth rate in Malaysia, which has actually fallen to less than 2%. At this rate the population will only be 24 million by the year 2010.

Nigeria

Like other West African countries, population growth continues at over 3% each year. At this rate the population will double in 25 years. There is no effective government plan to control the birth rate. Any economic growth is eaten up by increasing numbers of people, and in the past decade national income has actually shrunk by 1.3% each year. Coupled with the expanding population, this means that the standard of living for the average Nigerian has fallen by nearly 50% over the decade.

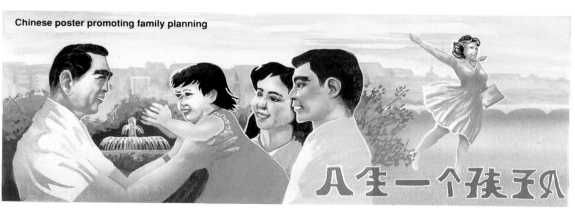

Chinese poster promoting family planning

人生一个孩子好

36

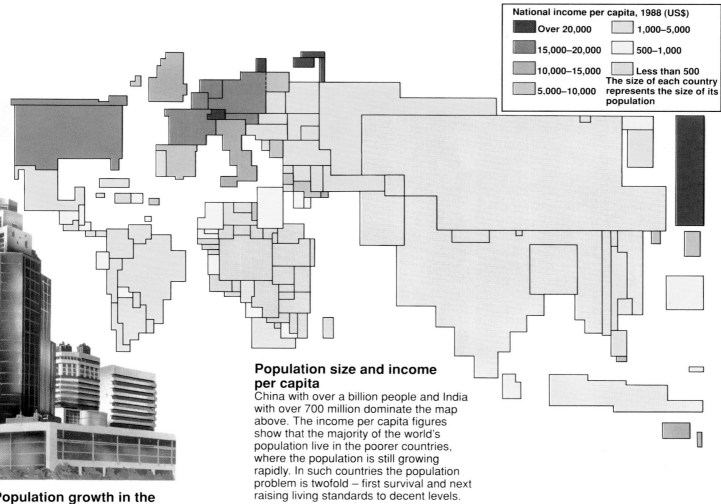

National income per capita, 1988 (US$)

■ Over 20,000	▦ 1,000–5,000
▨ 15,000–20,000	□ 500–1,000
▨ 10,000–15,000	□ Less than 500
▨ 5,000–10,000	The size of each country represents the size of its population

Population size and income per capita

China with over a billion people and India with over 700 million dominate the map above. The income per capita figures show that the majority of the world's population live in the poorer countries, where the population is still growing rapidly. In such countries the population problem is twofold – first survival and next raising living standards to decent levels.

Population growth in the long run

The charts below show two perspectives in population change. The first shows a population explosion after the year 1750, while the second divides population change in the very long run into three eras of economic activity. To achieve a stable population in the industrial era, without an enormous increase in death rates, there must be a reduction in birth rates.

World population 9000BC–AD2000

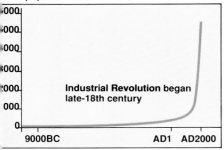

Industrial Revolution began late-18th century

9000BC   AD1   AD2000

World population 1 million BC–AD2050

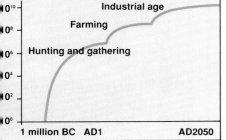

Industrial age

Farming

Hunting and gathering

10^{10}
10^8
10^6
10^4
10^2
10^0

1 million BC   AD1   AD2050

Education in Malawi

The education that people need to fulfil their potential and raise their incomes is often not available in countries with rapid population growth, such as Malawi. Because the school aged population grows very quickly, education has to be spread more thinly or the cost of providing it escalates. The World Bank has shown the savings that could be made if the birth rate was reduced. Such savings could be used to improve the standard of education by reducing class sizes and increasing enrollment.

Malawi primary school costs

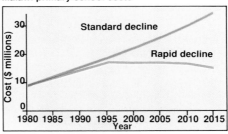

Standard decline

Rapid decline

Cost ($ millions)
30
20
10
0

1980 1985 1990 1995 2000 2005 2010 2015
Year

Standard decline: costs with current trend in birth rate

Rapid decline: costs with effective birth control program

Although enrollments are low, class sizes in Malawi are over 60 pupils per teacher.

17 Economic Growth

There are only two ways to improve people's standard of living: redistribution (cutting the economic 'cake' in a different way – see INCOME INEQUALITY) and growth (making the cake bigger). Growth requires investment in productive facilities like factories, power stations and railways. The more investment, the greater the rate of growth is likely to be. But more investment can only be achieved by having less consumption. Thus, high growth means giving up some consumption now, in the hope of having greater consumption possibilities in the future.

Economic growth is usually measured in terms of percentage changes in the Gross National Product (GNP) per person. The GNP is the value of all the goods and services produced in a country in a year. On its own, this measure cannot tell us how well off the average citizen is. For that, we need to know the GNP *per person*. Growth in the GNP per person tells us how things are changing for the average citizen. If a country's population is growing faster than its economy, the GNP per person will be decreasing (so the percentage change will be negative). If the economy is growing faster than the population (which implies a positive percentage change in the GNP per person), the standard of living of the average citizen will be improving. The way income is distributed will, of course, determine which groups of citizens actually benefit from this growth.

Closing the development gap
The development gap between two countries will close provided the growth rate of the lower income country is larger than that of the higher income country. The bigger the difference in the growth rates, the faster the gap will close. The graph (right) shows that South Korea will catch up with Australia in 24 years if present rates continue.

The average income per capita in the high income countries as a whole is more than 50 times higher than that of the low income countries as a whole. If the difference in the growth rates between these two groups over the past 25 years were to be maintained, it would take 500 years for the poor countries to catch up. However, it is highly unlikely that growth rate differences will remain stable for 50

Sustainable growth
Economic growth means more economic activity, and more activity means more pollution and resource consumption. Growth is vital for improving living standards, but if resources are eaten up too fast it is unlikely to be sustainable; the drive for growth may eventually collapse as resources become increasingly scarce and hard to exploit. The drain on the world's resources that could result from, say, Chad or China catching up with Canada in economic terms is illustrated in the bar chart.

Energy consumption per capita

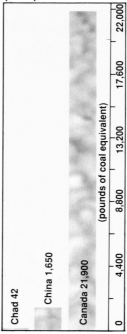

Chad 42   China 1,650   Canada 21,900

(pounds of coal equivalent)

years, let alone 500. In any case, growth rate averages conceal a great deal of variation. In at least 11 of the world's poorest countries, the past 25 years has been a period of negative growth or shrinkage in the GNP per capita and here, the poor are getting poorer not just relatively, but absolutely.

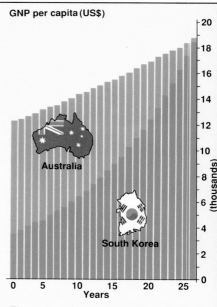

GNP per capita (US$)

Australia

South Korea

Years

The average Australian is 3.5 times better off than the average South Korean. But the South Korean economy is growing 4 times as fast.

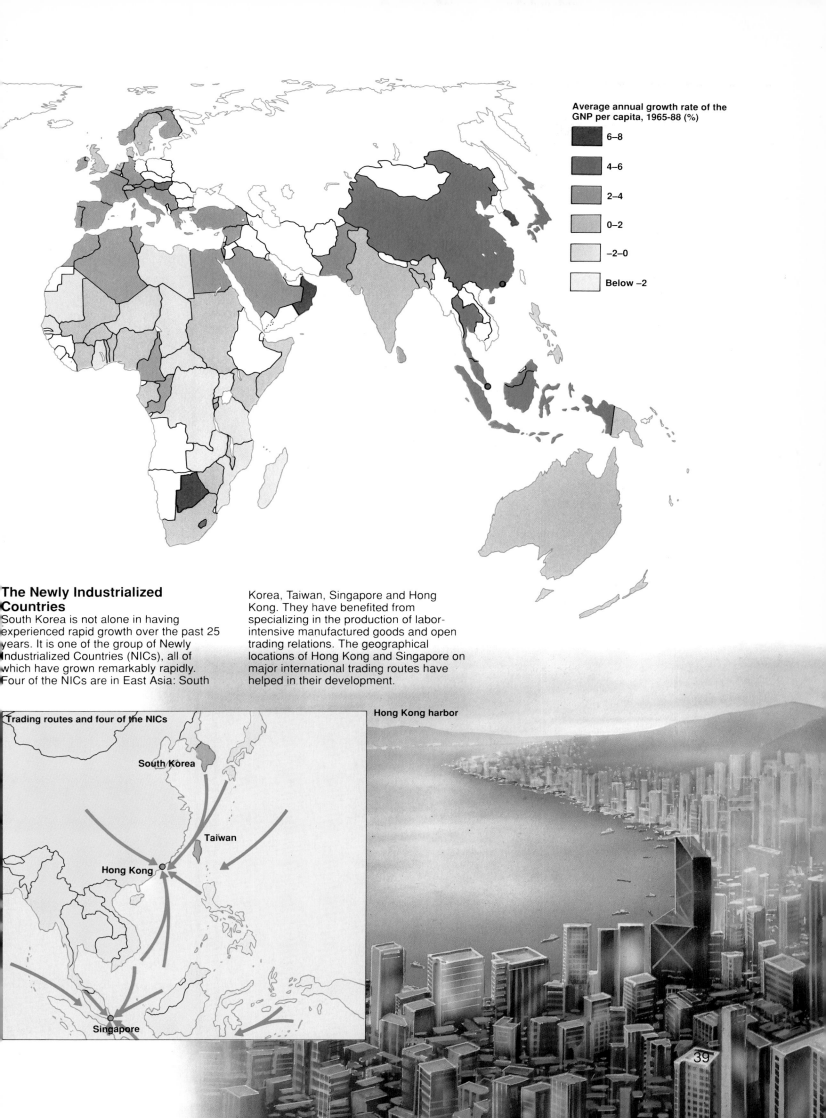

The Newly Industrialized Countries

South Korea is not alone in having experienced rapid growth over the past 25 years. It is one of the group of Newly Industrialized Countries (NICs), all of which have grown remarkably rapidly. Four of the NICs are in East Asia: South Korea, Taiwan, Singapore and Hong Kong. They have benefited from specializing in the production of labor-intensive manufactured goods and open trading relations. The geographical locations of Hong Kong and Singapore on major international trading routes have helped in their development.

Trading routes and four of the NICs

South Korea

Taiwan

Hong Kong

Singapore

Hong Kong harbor

39

18 Development

Economic development is not the same as economic growth. Development tends to be associated with growth per capita but it involves much more than that. In particular, it involves improvements in human welfare. The map (right) shows the development of countries in terms of a new measure devised by the United Nations Development Program, called the Human Development Index. This index brings together life expectancy, literacy and income per capita. With this measure, development is seen as a process which involves people living longer, being better educated and being better off economically.

Economic development is also associated with changes in economic structure (see below) and social and demographic structure (see below, right). To illustrate the idea of structural change in an economy, consider the case of Indonesia. In 1965, the economy of Indonesia was dominated by agriculture, which generated 56% of the country's output or Gross Domestic Product. Industry contributed only 13% and services 31%. By 1988, the structure of production had changed significantly. Only 24% of output came from agriculture, with 36% from industry and 40% from services. The difference in the volume of the Indonesia pie charts below illustrates the growth in total output (GDP) from 1965 to 1988. Taken together, the charts show development as a process of growth accompanied by structural change.

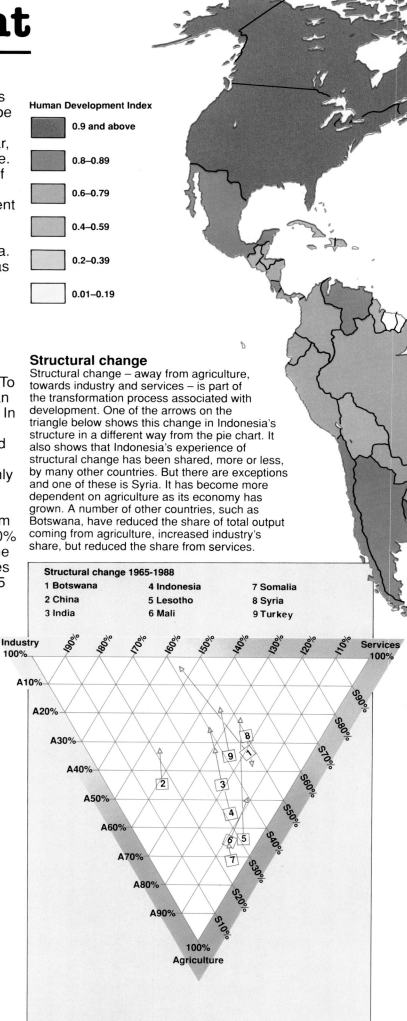

Human Development Index

- 0.9 and above
- 0.8–0.89
- 0.6–0.79
- 0.4–0.59
- 0.2–0.39
- 0.01–0.19

Structural change

Structural change – away from agriculture, towards industry and services – is part of the transformation process associated with development. One of the arrows on the triangle below shows this change in Indonesia's structure in a different way from the pie chart. It also shows that Indonesia's experience of structural change has been shared, more or less, by many other countries. But there are exceptions and one of these is Syria. It has become more dependent on agriculture as its economy has grown. A number of other countries, such as Botswana, have reduced the share of total output coming from agriculture, increased industry's share, but reduced the share from services.

Structural change 1965-1988

1 Botswana	4 Indonesia	7 Somalia
2 China	5 Lesotho	8 Syria
3 India	6 Mali	9 Turkey

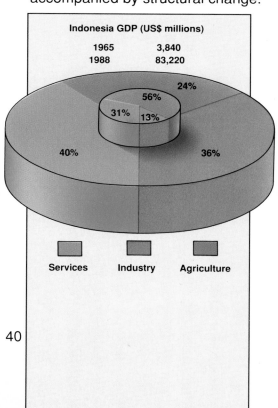

Indonesia GDP (US$ millions)

| 1965 | 3,840 |
| 1988 | 83,220 |

Services   Industry   Agriculture

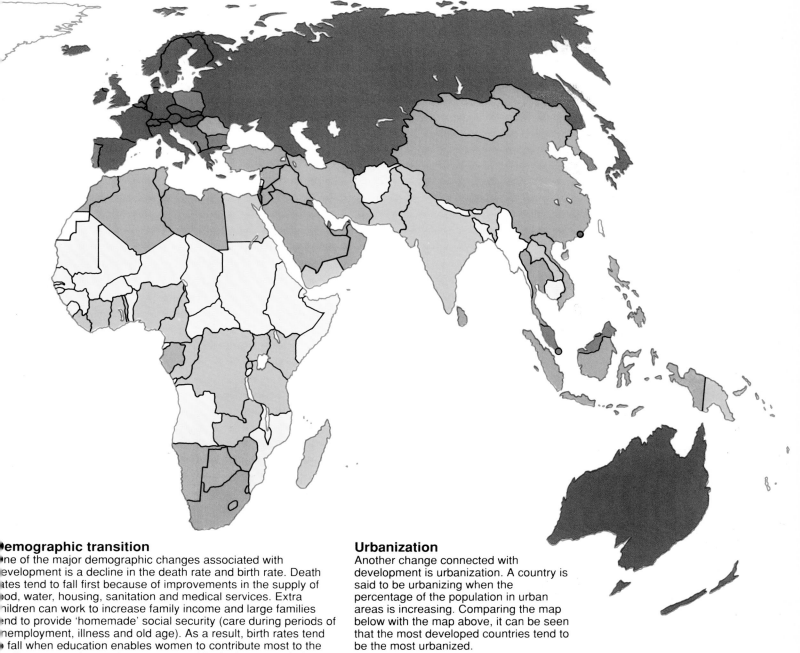

Demographic transition

One of the major demographic changes associated with development is a decline in the death rate and birth rate. Death rates tend to fall first because of improvements in the supply of food, water, housing, sanitation and medical services. Extra children can work to increase family income and large families tend to provide 'homemade' social security (care during periods of unemployment, illness and old age). As a result, birth rates tend to fall when education enables women to contribute most to the family economy by earning money outside the home, and when proper social security systems are in place. In practice, demographic processes are more complex than the graph suggests.

School enrollment

As countries develop, they tend to invest increasingly in education. A better educated population is a more productive population. Education can be thought of as a form of investment and is sometimes described as investment in human capital.

Urbanization

Another change connected with development is urbanization. A country is said to be urbanizing when the percentage of the population in urban areas is increasing. Comparing the map below with the map above, it can be seen that the most developed countries tend to be the most urbanized.

Birth and death rates

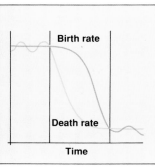

Secondary school enrollment ratios (%)

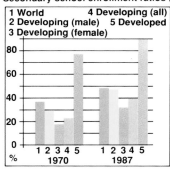

1 World   4 Developing (all)
2 Developing (male)   5 Developed
3 Developing (female)

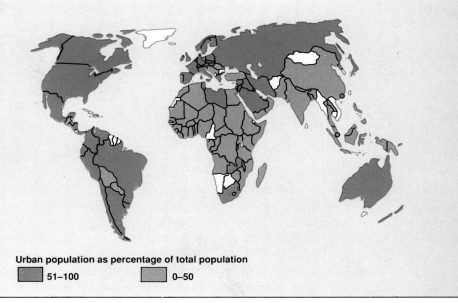

Urban population as percentage of total population

■ 51–100   ■ 0–50

19 Regional Imbalance

Income distribution within countries may be very uneven (see INCOME INEQUALITY) and often some parts of a country are poorer than others. This is called regional imbalance, and affected areas usually suffer from high unemployment, low growth and below average income per capita. The problem affects all countries, from the least to the most developed, and is often caused by structural change (see DEVELOPMENT). For example, the decline of traditional industries may damage regions where those industries are based (see MANUFACTURING).

Many policies have been tried by governments to reduce regional imbalance, but the problem is difficult to solve. The main ways in which governments try to promote growth in less developed regions include building transport links and locating government-owned industry within the region. Financial incentives may also be offered by the government to encourage private businesses to set up within the region.

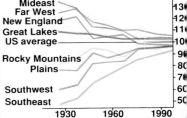

Rustbelt   Sunbelt

Far West
New England
Great Lakes
New York C
Michigan
Illinois   Ohio
Indiana
Plains   Mideast
Rocky Mountains
Southwest
Dallas   Southeast
Texas
Houston

Changing regional fortunes

The state of the national and international economy can affect regions differently. In the 1970s the 'rustbelt' of the US struggled, as high oil prices and world economic recession hurt the traditional manufacturing sector that was already in decline. In 1975, the headquarters of the rustbelt – New York City – went bankrupt. In contrast, the 'sunbelt' was booming, and oil-producing states like Texas grew rapidly as a result of high oil prices. By 1980, however, oil prices had fallen and cities like Houston and Dallas were in trouble. But New York City had bounced back, its financial services sector booming from the extensive economic borrowing of the 1970s. A downturn in 1981-82 hit hardest in the regions which still relied on traditional manufacturing,

such as Ohio, Michigan, Indiana and Illinois. The east and west coasts escaped from the worst effects of the downturn because of defense spending and a boom in property and financial services. In the 1990-91 recession, the financial and property sectors are struggling, and the coastal states are the most affected.

Income per capita (percentage of US average)

Mideast   130
Far West   120
New England   110
Great Lakes
US average   100
                    90
Rocky Mountains   80
Plains   70
                    60
Southwest   50
Southeast
        1930   1960   1990

GDP per capita, 1987 (Italy=100)

■	Over 130
■	110–130
■	90–110
■	70–90
□	Under 70

The north-south divide in Italy

Southern Italy (the Mezzogiorno) shows how an underdeveloped region can persist in an advanced industrial country. The government has spent a lot of money on the Mezzogiorno and many state-controlled companies producing steel, oil, chemicals and textiles were established in the south. Private businesses were encouraged to set up there through loans from the government and other incentives. Despite these efforts, the north-south gap is as wide as it was 40 years ago. Higher wages in the north have led to a massive migration northwards, and businesses have preferred to expand in the established north rather than set up in the south. It is hoped, however, that new plans to help small and medium sized businesses will speed up economic development in the south.

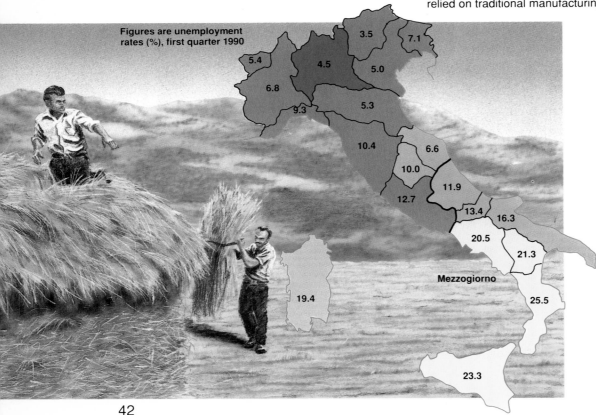

Figures are unemployment rates (%), first quarter 1990

3.5   7.1
5.4   4.5   5.0
6.8
9.3   5.3
10.4   6.6
10.0
12.7   11.9
13.4   16.3
20.5
21.3
Mezzogiorno
19.4
25.5
23.3

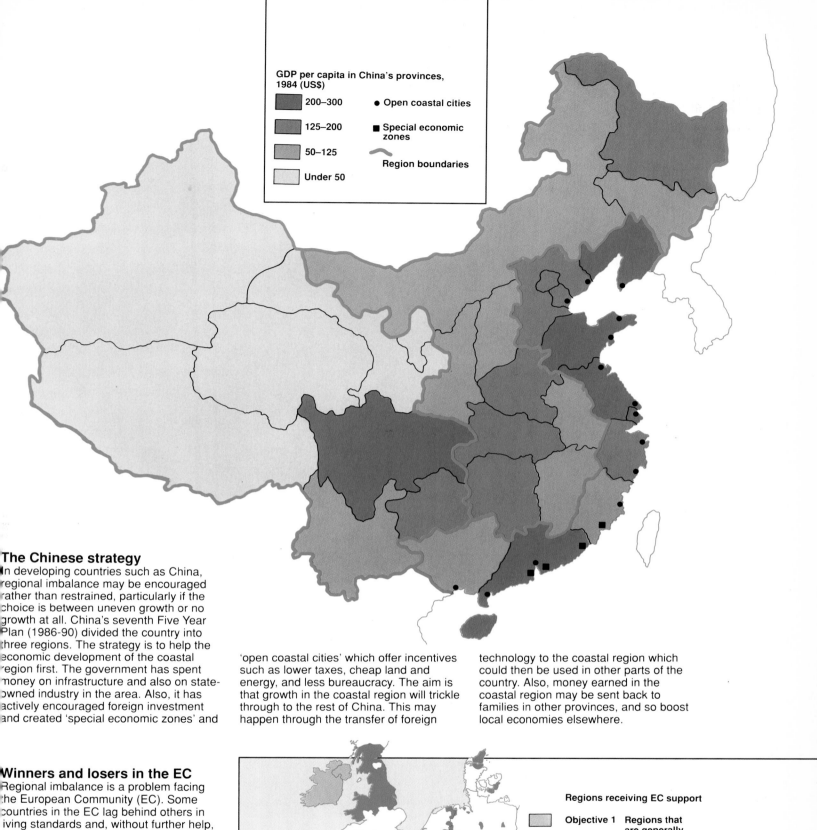

GDP per capita in China's provinces, 1984 (US$)

- 200–300
- 125–200
- 50–125
- Under 50

● Open coastal cities

■ Special economic zones

〰 Region boundaries

The Chinese strategy

In developing countries such as China, regional imbalance may be encouraged rather than restrained, particularly if the choice is between uneven growth or no growth at all. China's seventh Five Year Plan (1986-90) divided the country into three regions. The strategy is to help the economic development of the coastal region first. The government has spent money on infrastructure and also on state-owned industry in the area. Also, it has actively encouraged foreign investment and created 'special economic zones' and 'open coastal cities' which offer incentives such as lower taxes, cheap land and energy, and less bureaucracy. The aim is that growth in the coastal region will trickle through to the rest of China. This may happen through the transfer of foreign technology to the coastal region which could then be used in other parts of the country. Also, money earned in the coastal region may be sent back to families in other provinces, and so boost local economies elsewhere.

Winners and losers in the EC

Regional imbalance is a problem facing the European Community (EC). Some countries in the EC lag behind others in living standards and, without further help, their situation may get worse with the development of the single European market (see TRADE BARRIERS AND COMMON MARKETS). The EC recently agreed to double the money it spends on regional policy. The map shows the areas that will receive the most support.

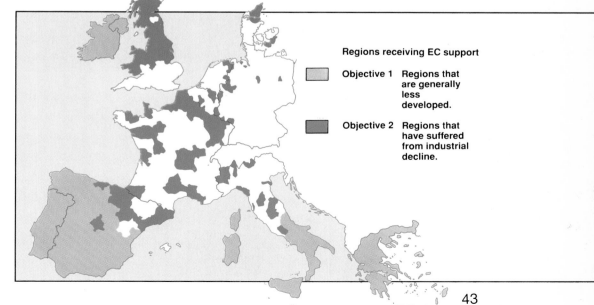

Regions receiving EC support

Objective 1 Regions that are generally less developed.

Objective 2 Regions that have suffered from industrial decline.

20 The Environment

The economy and the environment are intimately related. The environment supplies the economy with all its resources, including water, timber, minerals and oil, and has to absorb all its waste products, including pollutants from factory chimneys, farmland and sewage works. Economists have tended to think of the environment as an effectively unlimited source of resources and as an infinite sink for absorbing pollutants. That is, the atmosphere, forests, rivers and seas have been thought of as capable of absorbing all the rubbish the economy throws into them. But some economists have always argued that pollution damages the resource base upon which the economy depends. For example, disposing of waste gases from a power station by pumping them into the atmosphere does not get rid of them from an economy by putting them into the environment. Instead, it shifts them, via the environment, to another part of the economy. The waste gases generate acid rain which causes forest damage and, therefore, reduces the resources of the forestry industry. The map (see top right) shows the areas of rain forest destruction, desertification and acid deposition. It is important to note that all of these problems have economic causes and economic consequences, as do the problems of global warming and atmospheric ozone depletion.

The proposed site for the Three Gorges Dam

The Three Gorges Dam

In July 1991 there were disastrous floods in the lower Yangtze basin in China, affecting as many as 200 million people. The floods made it more likely that a long-term plan will be implemented to dam the Yangtze in the Three Gorges area. As well as providing much needed flood control to save people, homes and crops downstream, the dam would generate huge quantities of electricity to help China's developing industries. However, environmentalists warn that the project could be a disaster. Up to 1 million people would lose their homes to the reservoir behind the dam and 253 square miles of land would be lost, including two cities. The displaced people, most of whom are agricultural workers, would need new land requiring extensive forest clearance. Serious bank erosion, reservoir siltation and the loss of natural habitats are also feared.

The timber trade

About 3 billion tons of wood are consumed every year, half of it as fuel (see ENERGY). About 248 million tons are pulped to make paper, most of which is produced and consumed in the developed world. With increased investment in education in the developing world, the demand for paper will increase. Other forest products include plywood, softwoods and hardwoods. Tropical hardwoods are used for construction and for luxury items like fine furniture, panelling and parquet floors. Most hardwoods come from South East Asia and are consumed in Japan and Western Europe. Softwood forestry in Europe and North America involves replanting and careful harvesting to maintain the stock of trees. Tropical hardwood forestry is more like mineral extraction – there is little replanting so forest yields will not be sustainable in the long run.

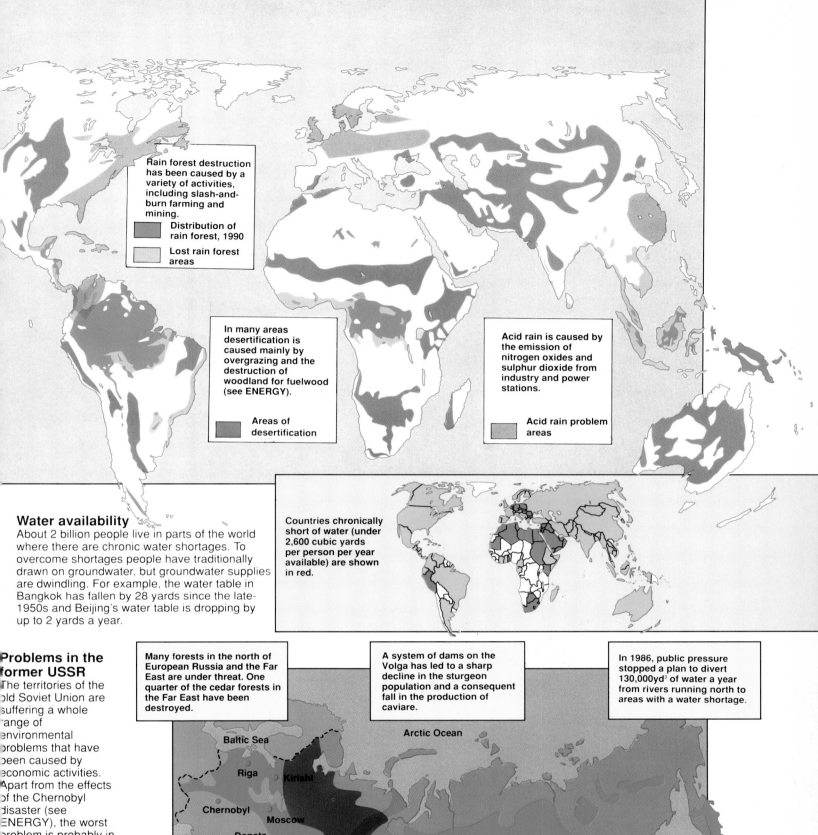

Rain forest destruction has been caused by a variety of activities, including slash-and-burn farming and mining.

◼ Distribution of rain forest, 1990

◻ Lost rain forest areas

In many areas desertification is caused mainly by overgrazing and the destruction of woodland for fuelwood (see ENERGY).

◼ Areas of desertification

Acid rain is caused by the emission of nitrogen oxides and sulphur dioxide from industry and power stations.

◻ Acid rain problem areas

Water availability

About 2 billion people live in parts of the world where there are chronic water shortages. To overcome shortages people have traditionally drawn on groundwater, but groundwater supplies are dwindling. For example, the water table in Bangkok has fallen by 28 yards since the late-1950s and Beijing's water table is dropping by up to 2 yards a year.

Countries chronically short of water (under 2,600 cubic yards per person per year available) are shown in red.

Problems in the former USSR

The territories of the old Soviet Union are suffering a whole range of environmental problems that have been caused by economic activities. Apart from the effects of the Chernobyl disaster (see ENERGY), the worst problem is probably in the area around the Aral Sea. Cotton growing in the region has consumed huge quantities of water causing the sea's level to fall by 14 yards. This has led to a collapse in the once thriving fishing industry and extensive damage to soils, crops and wildlife.

Many forests in the north of European Russia and the Far East are under threat. One quarter of the cedar forests in the Far East have been destroyed.

A system of dams on the Volga has led to a sharp decline in the sturgeon population and a consequent fall in the production of caviare.

In 1986, public pressure stopped a plan to divert 130,000yd³ of water a year from rivers running north to areas with a water shortage.

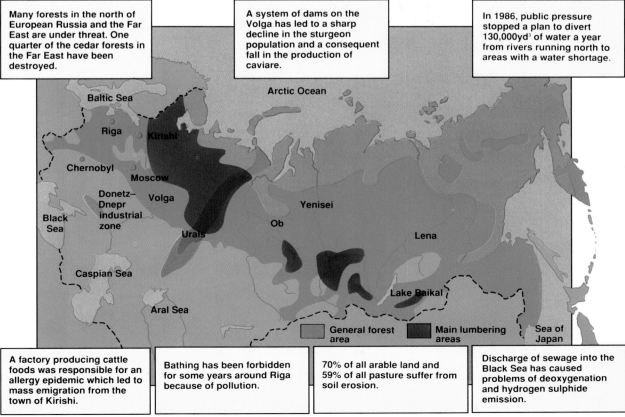

◻ General forest area   ◼ Main lumbering areas

A factory producing cattle foods was responsible for an allergy epidemic which led to mass emigration from the town of Kirishi.

Bathing has been forbidden for some years around Riga because of pollution.

70% of all arable land and 59% of all pasture suffer from soil erosion.

Discharge of sewage into the Black Sea has caused problems of deoxygenation and hydrogen sulphide emission.

21 Unemployment

Not everyone in a population wants to work or is able to work. Those who do want to work are called the work force. Unemployment exists when members of the work force cannot find work. There are three types of unemployment: structural unemployment, which is due in part to mismatches between the skills available and the skills required; seasonal unemployment, which occurs when certain jobs are available for only part of the year; and cyclical unemployment, which occurs when an economy suffers one of its periodic downturns. There tend to be wide variations in the unemployment rates for men and women, for different regions and for different types of workers. Most people who become unemployed get jobs again fairly quickly but some remain on unemployment registers for months or years. Older people in depressed regions with the wrong sort of skills for the jobs available are the most vulnerable.

Unemployment figures for 1990 for the OECD (industrialized market) economies are shown above. Unemployment data is available for other countries, but much of it is unreliable. However, many countries in the developing world have very serious unemployment problems. The latest unemployment estimate for Niger, for example, is around 50%. Among the OECD countries, the worst unemployment in 1990 was Spain's at 16.1%.

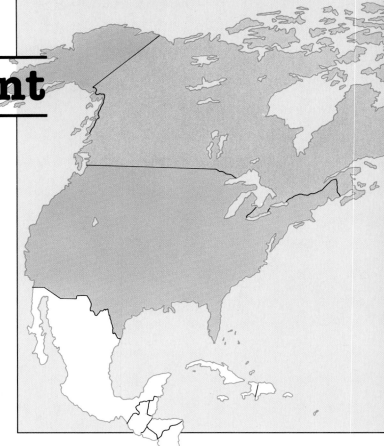

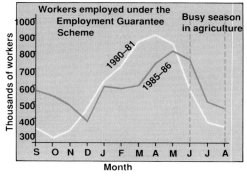

Workers employed under the Employment Guarantee Scheme · Busy season in agriculture · Thousands of workers · 1980–81 · 1985–86 · S O N D J F M A M J J A · Month

India's Employment Guarantee Scheme

In addition to the medium-term ups and downs associated with the business cycle, most economies suffer from problems of seasonal unemployment. In Britain, for example, seaside towns like Margate tend to have high unemployment rates during the winter off-season. In countries that rely heavily on agriculture, seasonal unemployment can be a particularly acute problem. In India, the Employment Guarantee Scheme (EGS), introduced in the early 1970s, attempts to provide employment for a standard wage within three miles of a participant's village. Such schemes can play a major part in helping to prevent famine (see POVERTY AND HUNGER).

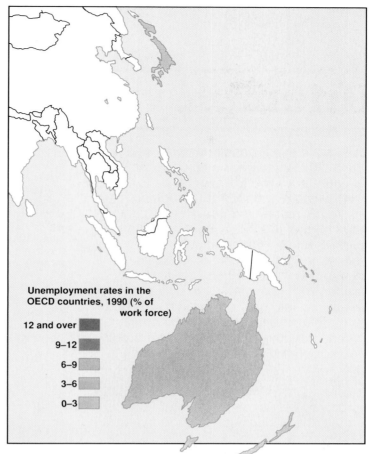

Unemployment rates in the OECD countries, 1990 (% of work force)

- 12 and over
- 9–12
- 6–9
- 3–6
- 0–3

Unemployment and technical change

One of the causes of unemployment is technical innovation. Businesses try to reduce production costs by introducing labor-saving devices. The number of people employed to build cars has fallen significantly with the introduction of robot welding and other automated devices. Newspapers have shed large numbers of printers with the advent of computerized typesetting. Even the lighthouse keeper is not safe. In 1991, Trinity House, which is responsible for all the lighthouses around the UK, announced that the jobs of all lighthouse keepers were to be phased out with the introduction of automatic lighthouse systems.

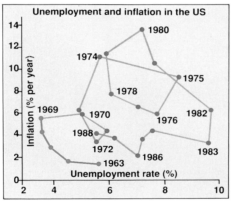

Unemployment and inflation in the US

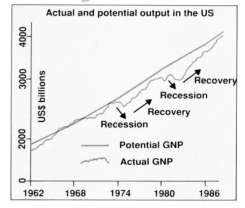

Actual and potential output in the US

Unemployment and inflation in the United States

There appears to be a close link between unemployment and inflation. The red line on the graph shows that in the US, between 1963 and 1969, there was a steady reduction in unemployment at the expense of an increase in inflation. By 1973, both unemployment and inflation had increased, although productivity had recovered. A mixture of government policies and the oil price shock in 1973 (see ENERGY) brought a deep recession that was followed by a rapid recovery, pushing inflation back up between 1976 and 1979. The second big rise in oil prices drove inflation to a peak in 1980. Once again, anti-inflationary policies caused unemployment to rise, reaching a maximum of nearly 10% in 1982. Since then, unemployment has fallen fairly steadily.

Unemployment and the business cycle

Cyclical unemployment is associated with the ups and downs of the economy over a period of years. In the late-1960s the American economy was working at its maximum capacity with full employment. Since then, it has experienced a number of downturns (recessions) and upturns (recoveries). When an economy is recovering or expanding, unemployment falls and more overtime is worked. The extra demand for labor tends to push wages up and, as a result, prices. Inflationary pressures build up (see INFLATION). To control inflation, governments tend to take measures that depress demand for goods and services. In turn, this leads to a lower output and lower demand for labor, so unemployment goes up.

22 Inflation

Inflation, which means continually rising prices, is the third great macroeconomic issue; the other two are growth and unemployment. Inflation is unpopular because rising prices mean that people cannot buy as much, so their standard of living falls unless they can get a compensating wage increase. But wage increases push up production costs and, as a result, product prices. Consequently, while wage increases for some households can help them to cope with the problem of inflation, they can also increase the problem for other people.

Some economists argue that inflation will not happen if the supply of money in the economy is kept under tight control. Others think that the underlying cause of inflation is not the money supply, but the persistently high demand for goods and services, and the labor that produces them. They tend to argue that controlling inflation requires agreements between government, unions and businesses to limit wage and price rises.

Inflation in Latin America

Inflation is a major problem in Latin America. The highest average rates in 1984-89 were in Nicaragua, Argentina, Brazil and Bolivia. Chile now has a fairly low inflation rate but in the 1970s it was over 100% per year. To reduce inflation, Chile adopted very tough monetary, tax and government spending policies which caused a good deal of suffering, especially amongst the poor. In an attempt to avoid the worst effects of such policies, Argentina and Brazil adopted different strategies, involving a mixture of wage and price controls, monetary reforms and other measures.

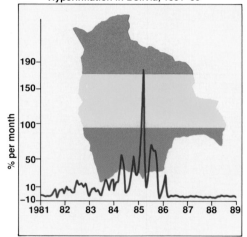

Hyperinflation in Bolivia, 1981–89

Inflation in Yugoslavia

Hyperinflation often follows conflict (see right), but major inflations can also precede conflicts. Inflation in China was one of the causes of the discontent that led to the massacre in Tiananmen Square. The civil war in Yugoslavia in 1991 was fuelled by major inflationary problems in the late 1980s. The two illustrations of the Yugoslav bank note represent the shrinkage in the purchasing power of the Yugoslav dinar in 1988-89.

The reduced value of the Yugoslav dinar

1988

1989

Hyperinflation

Extremely high inflation (typically taken to mean a rate of more than 1,000% per year) is called hyperinflation. Some of the worst experiences of hyperinflation have occurred after wars. At the height of the hyperinflation in Germany in 1922-23, an item costing the equivalent of $1 at the start of the month, cost $290 at the end. Among many other stories of hyperinflation, one is of a woman who went shopping with a basket full of money. She put the basket down for a moment and it was stolen, but the virtually worthless money that had been in it was left behind. The graph shows the course of hyperinflation in Bolivia, with inflation expressed as a percentage increase in prices per month. A major part of the cause of this hyperinflation was the Bolivian government's attempt to get out of economic trouble by printing more and more money.

With hyperinflation, money loses its effectiveness as a means of exchange.

48

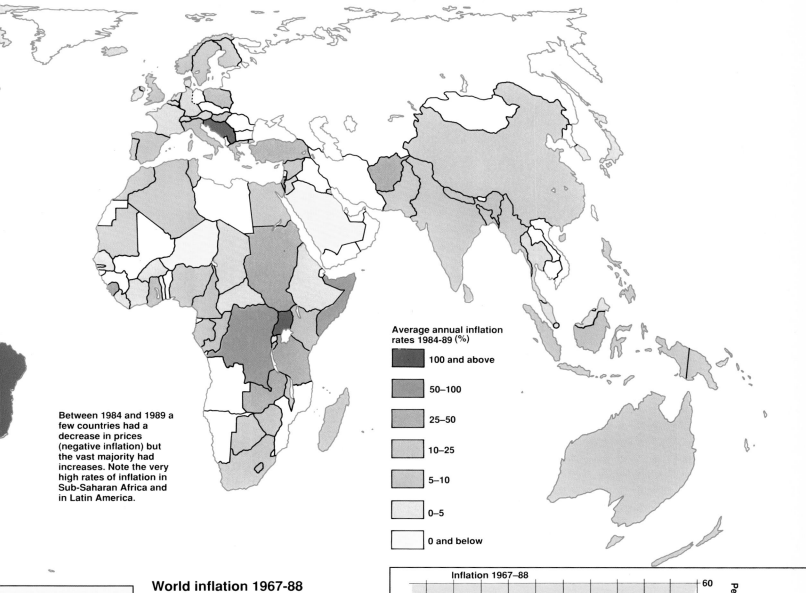

Average annual inflation
rates 1984-89 (%)

- 100 and above
- 50–100
- 25–50
- 10–25
- 5–10
- 0–5
- 0 and below

Between 1984 and 1989 a few countries had a decrease in prices (negative inflation) but the vast majority had increases. Note the very high rates of inflation in Sub-Saharan Africa and in Latin America.

World inflation 1967-88

Inflation has been worse for the developing than the developed world throughout this period. The sharp rise in inflation in the early 1970s was due to a combination of events, including the dramatic increase in the price of oil (see ENERGY), the abandonment of the so-called Bretton Woods agreement under which the value of the US dollar was fixed to the price of gold (see THE WORLD FINANCIAL SYSTEM), and poor harvests all over the world. After another peak in 1980 following the second major increase in oil prices, inflation in the developed world has decreased.

Inflation in the 1980s

The graph illustrates some recent high inflation experiences. Over the period shown, Israel and Bolivia had notable success in reducing very high inflation rates. The two major problems with inflation are that it devalues people's savings and makes the whole economy inefficient. Instead of an efficient pattern of weekly shopping, people go to the store frequently to try to beat the ever-rising prices. Similarly, instead of a weekly visit to the bank, people go daily or even hourly to get currency. Thus, very high inflation soon creates economic chaos, and stabilization becomes vital.

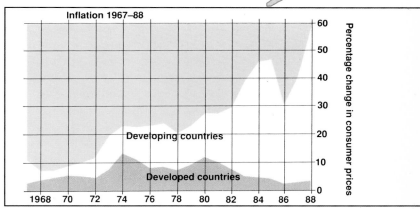

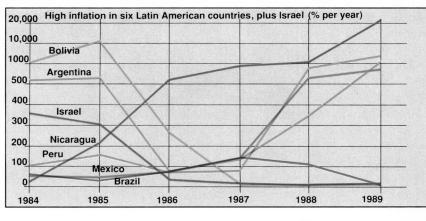

49

23 The World Financial System

Money travels around the globe in greater quantities and at faster speeds than ever before. It takes a host of forms, including currency, investments, savings, government bonds and even debt swaps. After World War II the major industrial powers set up a number of institutions to regulate their economies: the World Bank to lend money for reconstructing damaged economies; the International Monetary Fund to help economies in trouble; and the General Agreement on Tariffs and Trade to open up and regulate world trade. The industrial powers also pegged their currencies to the US dollar, which in turn was backed up by gold reserves, thus providing stable exchange rates.

In the early 1970s this system began to go wrong, Japan and West Germany challenged US leadership of the world economy, leading to the removal of the dollar from the gold standard in 1971. This allowed currencies to float against each other, destabilizing exchange rates. The situation worsened with the large increase in the price of oil in 1973 and the world's economy went into recession. However, conditions eventually improved and financial markets now operate 24 hours a day and since 1982 profits on trading of all kinds have shot up. However, this system means that any one government now has less control over its own economy, and that any collapse circulates the globe very rapidly.

Stock exchanges

A stock exchange, or 'bourse,' is a market in which businesses raise fresh capital from investors looking for profits. This is done by issuing or floating shares in the company, the value of which depends upon its subsequent economic performance. These shares or equities may also be traded among investors.

Governments also use stock exchanges to raise money by issuing bonds and gilts which pay back at given rates of interest. All pieces of interest-bearing paper, which include many other types of investment, are known as securities. The world's largest exchanges are New York, Tokyo and London, whose opening times together cover the whole 24 hours of each day. Their performance is shown in indexes such as the Dow Jones (New York) or Nikkei (Tokyo) which summarizes the ups and downs of a number of key companies.

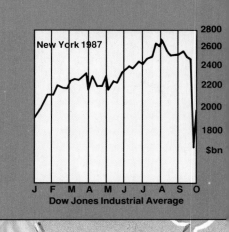

New York 1987
Dow Jones Industrial Average

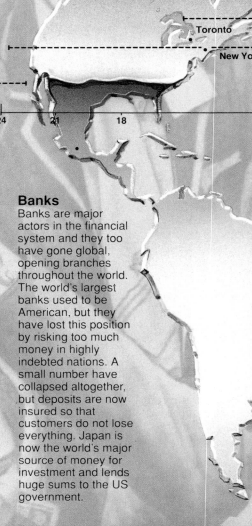

Toronto
New Yo
24   21   18

Banks

Banks are major actors in the financial system and they too have gone global, opening branches throughout the world. The world's largest banks used to be American, but they have lost this position by risking too much money in highly indebted nations. A small number have collapsed altogether, but deposits are now insured so that customers do not lose everything. Japan is now the world's major source of money for investment and lends huge sums to the US government.

Exchange rates and Euromarkets

Tourists like to know how much foreign money they can buy with their own, while an industrialist needs to know how much imported materials will cost and how much to charge for exports. Unless the rates of exchange between currencies are fairly stable, both tourists and business people cannot plan ahead easily. But since the 1970s such rates have fluctuated a lot, especially the US dollar. Such changes in currency values allow people to speculate in them, in what are known as Euromarkets. London, Singapore, Nassau (in the Bahamas), Hong Kong and Luxembourg are the major centers. Such speculation can make a government's task very difficult, particularly if it has to intervene with its own money to maintain the value of its currency.

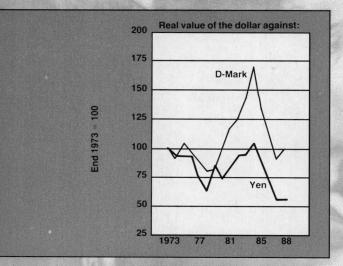

Real value of the dollar against:
End 1973 = 100
D-Mark
Yen
1973 77 81 85 88

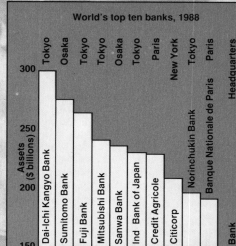

World's top ten banks, 1988
Assets ($ billions)
Dai-Ichi Kangyo Bank — Tokyo
Sumitomo Bank — Osaka
Fuji Bank — Tokyo
Mitsubishi Bank — Tokyo
Sanwa Bank — Osaka
Ind. Bank of Japan — Tokyo
Credit Agricole — Paris
Citicorp — New York
Norinchukin Bank — Tokyo
Banque Nationale de Paris — Paris
Bank — Headquarters

London 1987
2400
2200
2000
1800
1700
$bn
J F M A M J J A S O
FT–SE 100 Index   Jan 3, 1984 = 1000

Tokyo 1987
26000
24000
22000
18000
1500
Ybn
J F M A M J J A S O
Nikkei Index   May 16, 1949 = 100

• Major stock exchanges

London
Paris
Frankfurt
Zurich

Opening hours of foreign exchange markets

12   9   6   3   0
Hours GMT   Hong Kong   Tokyo

Singapore/Malaysia

Sydney

Black Monday 1987

Coming out of the recession in 1982 the world's stock markets enjoyed record trading and profits, a situation known as a 'bull market.' The United States' 47 million shareholders (27% of all adults) and the UK's 9 million (20% of all adults) reaped big financial gains on their investments. But on Monday, 19 October 1987, in a shock wave which sped through the world's markets (see the graphs above), shares suffered record falls. American investors lost $1 trillion. The underlying cause may have been a lack of confidence in the US economy and a feeling that the bull market had to stop some time. But computers which automatically respond to falling share prices by selling probably intensified the process. There were fears of a repeat of the dreadful Wall Street Crash of 1929 which plunged the world into its worst depression. In fact, as big as the fall was, it simply wiped out a year's worth of gains, but Tokyo investors still finished the year with small profits.

USA

Japan

UK

Germany

Canada

France

Switzerland

Australia

Netherlands

Sweden

Hong Kong

Spain

Singapore

Belgium

Denmark

South Africa

% of total world market in equities

Largest stock exchanges (by country)

24 Foreign Debt

A major economic problem is the enormous debt owed by developing countries to banks and governments in the developed world. Developing countries borrowed heavily in the 1970s with the active encouragement of the developed world. It was expected that investments would lead to growth, enabling the loans to be repaid. But a downturn in the world's economy left many developing countries with huge debts and falling incomes. This has forced them to reduce the standard of living of their populations, causing increased poverty. The problem of repayment has created instability in the world banking system. It is in the interest of all parties, therefore, to sort out the problem and enable developing countries to expand their economies.

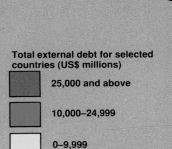

Total external debt for selected countries (US$ millions)

- 25,000 and above
- 10,000–24,999
- 0–9,999
- ▲ Countries whose external debt is greater than their GNP
- N.A.

Interest rates

Interest rates on loans to developing countries

%
20
15
10
5
0
–5
–10

1976 1979 1982 1985 1987

All loans have interest rates, representing the cost of borrowing the money. Each 1% rise in interest rates adds $1 billion to Brazil's debt and $500 million to Argentina's. In 1988 Argentina exported $8.5 billion of goods, which was $3 billion more than it imported. But its interest payments were $4.7 billion. Until these sums are paid, the country cannot even begin to clear the original loans.

Net flow from developing to developed countries, 1982–87 = $93 billion

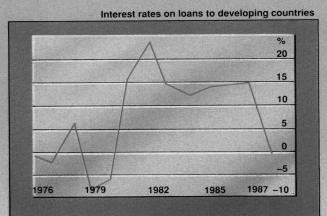

World debt crisis

1. 1973-1974 The Organization of Petroleum Exporting Countries (OPEC) quadruples the price of oil. Money from the oil-importing countries flows into the oil-exporting countries (see left).
2. The oil-exporters either lend the money to developing countries, or place it in banks in the industrial countries (see left).
3. 1974-1982 The industrial economies are growing slowly and there is little demand for the new money. The developing countries want funds for development projects (see left).
4. 1979-1982 The world economy slows down; the price of oil doubles in 1979, interest rates on loans go up, prices of Third World exports fall. The debt burden increases so that more money is flowing out of the

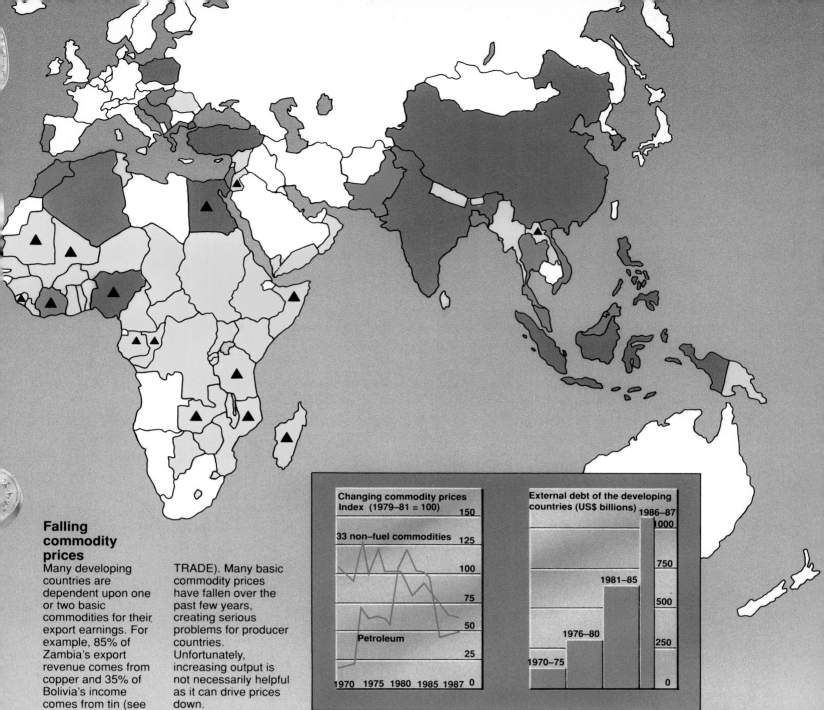

Falling commodity prices

Many developing countries are dependent upon one or two basic commodities for their export earnings. For example, 85% of Zambia's export revenue comes from copper and 35% of Bolivia's income comes from tin (see TRADE). Many basic commodity prices have fallen over the past few years, creating serious problems for producer countries. Unfortunately, increasing output is not necessarily helpful as it can drive prices down.

Changing commodity prices
Index (1979–81 = 100)

33 non–fuel commodities

Petroleum

1970 1975 1980 1985 1987

(values: 150, 125, 100, 75, 50, 25, 0)

External debt of the developing countries (US$ billions)

1986–87
1981–85
1976–80
1970–75

(values: 1000, 750, 500, 250, 0)

developing world in repayments than flowing in as aid (see right).
5. 1982 Mexico refuses to pay interest on its loans. The Western banks panic.
6. The International Monetary Fund (IMF) steps in to restructure over 50 indebted economies. They oblige governments to cut public expenditure.
7. 1985 Peru decides to limit repayment of debt to 10% of the value of its exports. The US government co-ordinates a rescue plan between the banks and the 15 highly-indebted countries.
8. 1986 Riots in Zambia as the government puts up the price of corn by 120% in order to pay back interest on loans.
9. 1987 Brazil suspends repayment of its debt for a year. The major Western banks set aside funds to cover possible losses resulting from non-payment of debt.
10. 1987-1988 The banks and the debtors get together to try to resolve the debt crisis.
11. 1990 The Brady Plan is implemented by the US government. Mexico receives a 35% debt reduction and its economy soon shows signs of recovery.

Net flow from developed to developing countries, 1982–87 = $61 billion

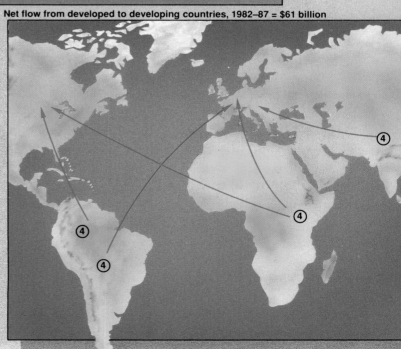

25 Aid

Foreign aid involves a transfer of resources from rich to poor countries. It takes many forms. Food aid helps reduce the suffering caused by famine (see POVERTY AND HUNGER), if it is in time and enough can be distributed. Medical assistance, such as immunization against preventable diseases, improves the health of the population of the receiving country, allowing the work force to be more productive. The transfer of vital technology to developing countries helps to promote economic growth, perhaps by increasing agricultural yields or establishing a new industry. The most important form of foreign aid is financial assistance, which may be a grant or low interest loan to allow the government of a receiving country to buy imports or fund public sector investment which it could not otherwise afford.

The effectiveness of foreign aid has been questioned. One problem is that aid donors may be motivated by considerations other than reducing poverty and promoting economic development in receiving countries. For strategic and commercial reasons, about 40% of total foreign aid goes to middle and high income countries, rather than to the poorest countries. Even where aid is directed to encourage the economic development of low income countries, the government policies may undermine the effect of the aid. One common example is the high proportion of government spending on defense in developing countries which hinders efforts to break the cycle of poverty. This is sometimes encouraged by the provision of military hardware and training by donor countries.

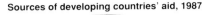
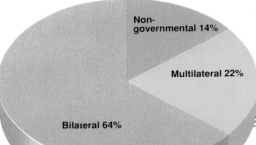

Sources of developing countries' aid, 1987

Non-governmental 14%

Multilateral 22%

Bilateral 64%

Aid donors

Official aid may be given directly by one government to another (bilateral aid) or through inter-governmental organizations such as the World Bank (multilateral aid), which collect money from members for funding projects in developing countries. A significant amount of aid is also given by private voluntary organizations, which tend to concentrate on grass roots assistance to reduce poverty. Most aid comes from the members of the OECD Development Assistance Committee (DAC). Although the US remains the largest donor in absolute terms, it contributes less per capita than almost all other donors. In 1970 the United Nations set a target for foreign aid of 0.7% of national income. Only the Scandinavian countries, France and Saudi Arabia have met this standard.

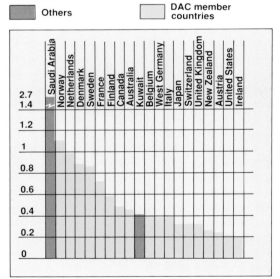

Help or hindrance?

For many developing countries, foreign aid represents a substantial fraction of national income. For some, aid is a much greater source of foreign currency than exports. Countries such as Indonesia and Korea have benefited greatly from aid, with assisted growth leading to reduced reliance on aid. Other countries, particularly in West Africa, have been caught in a vicious circle of dependence on aid. The motives for giving aid are varied. Bilateral aid may go to countries of strategical importance to the donor. For example, US aid has favored Egypt and Israel, which are US allies.

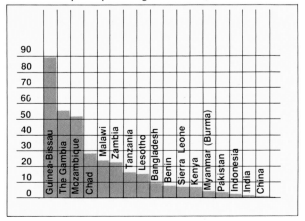

Total aid receipts as percentage of the GNP, 1987

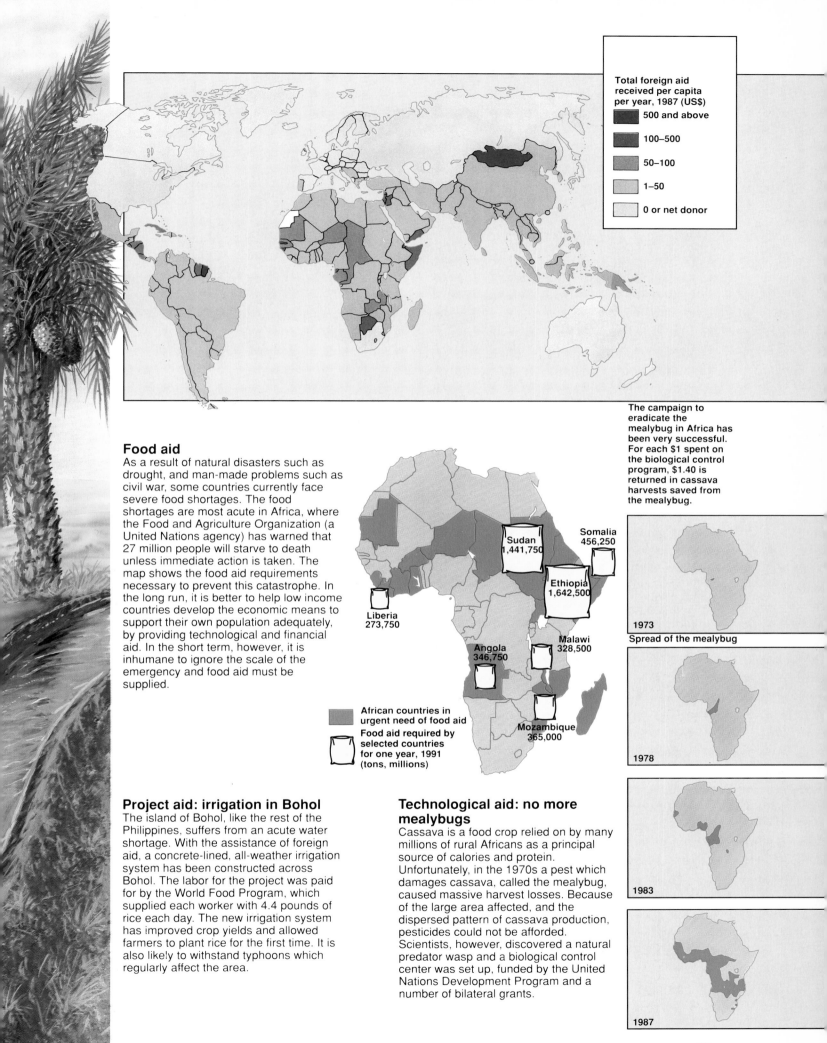

Total foreign aid received per capita per year, 1987 (US$)
- 500 and above
- 100–500
- 50–100
- 1–50
- 0 or net donor

Food aid

As a result of natural disasters such as drought, and man-made problems such as civil war, some countries currently face severe food shortages. The food shortages are most acute in Africa, where the Food and Agriculture Organization (a United Nations agency) has warned that 27 million people will starve to death unless immediate action is taken. The map shows the food aid requirements necessary to prevent this catastrophe. In the long run, it is better to help low income countries develop the economic means to support their own population adequately, by providing technological and financial aid. In the short term, however, it is inhumane to ignore the scale of the emergency and food aid must be supplied.

Sudan 1,441,750
Somalia 456,250
Ethiopia 1,642,500
Liberia 273,750
Malawi 328,500
Angola 346,750
Mozambique 365,000

African countries in urgent need of food aid

Food aid required by selected countries for one year, 1991 (tons, millions)

The campaign to eradicate the mealybug in Africa has been very successful. For each $1 spent on the biological control program, $1.40 is returned in cassava harvests saved from the mealybug.

1973
Spread of the mealybug

1978

1983

1987

Project aid: irrigation in Bohol

The island of Bohol, like the rest of the Philippines, suffers from an acute water shortage. With the assistance of foreign aid, a concrete-lined, all-weather irrigation system has been constructed across Bohol. The labor for the project was paid for by the World Food Program, which supplied each worker with 4.4 pounds of rice each day. The new irrigation system has improved crop yields and allowed farmers to plant rice for the first time. It is also likely to withstand typhoons which regularly affect the area.

Technological aid: no more mealybugs

Cassava is a food crop relied on by many millions of rural Africans as a principal source of calories and protein. Unfortunately, in the 1970s a pest which damages cassava, called the mealybug, caused massive harvest losses. Because of the large area affected, and the dispersed pattern of cassava production, pesticides could not be afforded. Scientists, however, discovered a natural predator wasp and a biological control center was set up, funded by the United Nations Development Program and a number of bilateral grants.

26 Trade

International trade is the sale of goods or services by one country to another. Countries can grow, mine or manufacture the things they are best at producing and sell them around the world (exports). With the money they earn, countries can buy the goods and services they need from other countries (imports). Producers who sell to local buyers often have an advantage over foreign producers because there are barriers to free trade between countries (see TRADE BARRIERS AND COMMON MARKETS). If the foreign product is cheap enough or good enough to get over these barriers, then trade can occur.

Generally, small countries depend more on trade than large ones, because they are less able to produce all that they need. In contrast, large countries such as the US, China and India depend less on trade. Because of the size of their economies, and especially their manufacturing industries, the OECD countries account for nearly three quarters of the world's trade. Trade is important for economic growth in both industrial and developing countries. A major problem that developing countries face is that they often rely on one main export. If the world price of this product falls, their economies immediately suffer. A country's strength as a trader is best measured by the difference between its exports and imports, known as the 'trade balance'. Recently, the US has imported far more than it has exported. This is called a 'trade deficit'. Because of the size of the US economy, the deficit has affected the whole world economy (see FOREIGN DEBT).

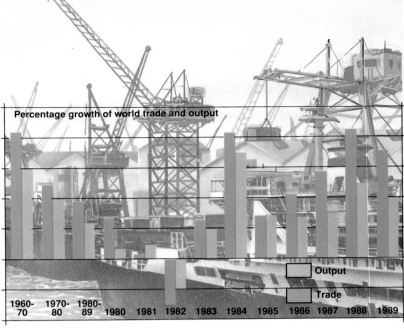

Percentage growth of world trade and output

| 1960-70 | 1970-80 | 1980-89 | 1980 | 1981 | 1982 | 1983 | 1984 | 1985 | 1986 | 1987 | 1988 | 1989 |

Output
Trade

The global economy
Trade is a major driving force behind economic growth.

Apart from such occasions as the world recession of 1981-82, trade has grown faster than the national product since World War II. The flow of trade means that the countries of the world are closely tied.

Dependence on one export
Many developing countries rely on one major export. This export is nearly alwa[ys] agricultural produce or raw materials. T[his] is risky because the price of such good[s] often unstable.

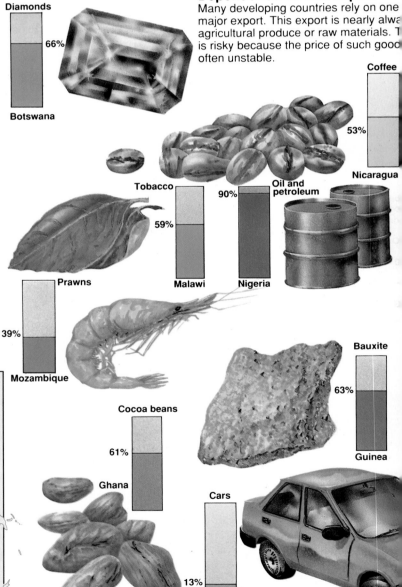

Diamonds
66%
Botswana

Coffee
53%
Nicaragua

Tobacco
59%
Malawi

Oil and petroleum
90%
Nigeria

Prawns
39%
Mozambique

Bauxite
63%
Guinea

Cocoa beans
61%
Ghana

Cars
13%
Japan

Major exports in selected countries as percentages of total exports

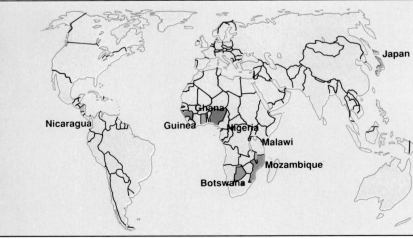

Japan
Nicaragua
Ghana
Guinea
Nigeria
Malawi
Mozambique
Botswana

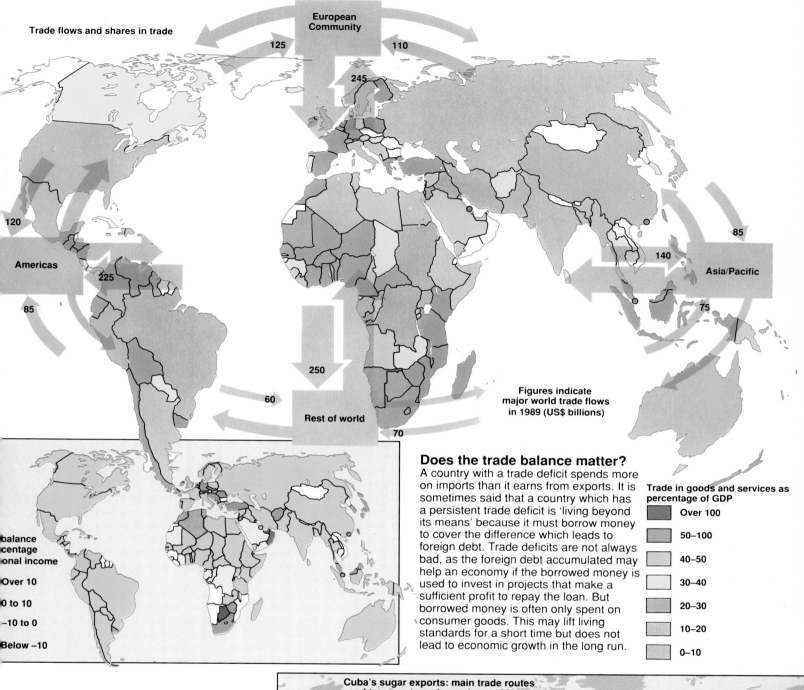

Trade flows and shares in trade

European Community

125   110

245

120

Americas

225

85

Asia/Pacific

85

140

75

250

60

Rest of world

70

Figures indicate
major world trade flows
in 1989 (US$ billions)

Trade balance as percentage of national income

Over 10

0 to 10

–10 to 0

Below –10

Does the trade balance matter?

A country with a trade deficit spends more on imports than it earns from exports. It is sometimes said that a country which has a persistent trade deficit is 'living beyond its means' because it must borrow money to cover the difference which leads to foreign debt. Trade deficits are not always bad, as the foreign debt accumulated may help an economy if the borrowed money is used to invest in projects that make a sufficient profit to repay the loan. But borrowed money is often only spent on consumer goods. This may lift living standards for a short time but does not lead to economic growth in the long run.

Trade in goods and services as percentage of GDP

Over 100

50–100

40–50

30–40

20–30

10–20

0–10

Cuban sugar trade

Cuba is by far the world's biggest exporter of sugar. Its trading partners show the influence of politics on trade. In 1959 Fidel Castro seized power in Cuba and the new socialist government took over all property owned by foreigners, including 36 sugar refineries owned by US companies. In retaliation, the US banned imports of Cuban sugar. To support a political ally, the USSR stepped in to buy Cuban sugar and paid prices that were good for Cuba. In this way Cuba was protected from world price changes. Following the upheavals in the USSR, support for Cuba was curtailed.

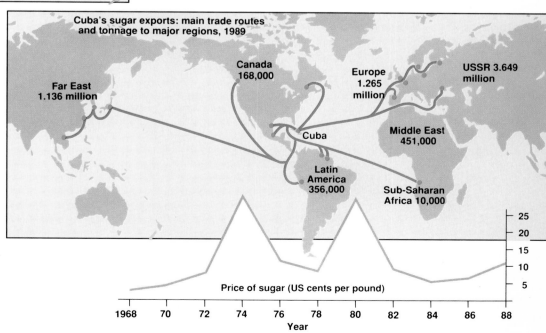

Cuba's sugar exports: main trade routes and tonnage to major regions, 1989

Canada
168,000

Europe
1.265
million

USSR 3.649
million

Far East
1.136 million

Cuba

Middle East
451,000

Latin
America
356,000

Sub-Saharan
Africa 10,000

Price of sugar (US cents per pound)

25
20
15
10
5

1968   70   72   74   76   78   80   82   84   86   88

Year

27 Trade Barriers and Common Markets

Trade barriers act as a brake on trade between countries. There are two types of barriers: natural and man-made. A major natural barrier is the distance between trading partners, which affects transport and communication costs. Because of advances in technology, these costs have fallen. Man-made barriers to trade are government policies that regulate trade, such as a 'tariff' which raises the price of imports and makes them less attractive to buy. A 'quota' is a limit on the number of imports. An 'export subsidy' is a government grant to producers to help them export.

All of these policies are widely used and their aim is to protect domestic producers against foreign competition. This protection hinders world trade and economic growth. Although reducing protection is desirable, a country might suffer if it were the only country to do so. As a result, it is important for countries to agree together to reduce trade barriers and promote free trade. This understanding led to the signing of the General Agreement on Tariffs and Trade (GATT) by many countries in 1947. Under the GATT, trade barriers have been steadily lowered. The desire to reduce trade barriers has also led to the formation of common markets around the world. Their aim is free trade between members and the best known is the European Community (EC).

Members of selected trading groups

- **EC** European Community
- **EFTA** European Free Trade Association
- **SADCC** Southern African Development Co-ordination Conference
- **ALADI** Asociación Latinoamericana de Integración
- **GCC** Gulf Co-operation Council
- **GATT** General Agreement on Tariffs and Trade (signatories and followers)

GATT gaps

The GATT has helped world trade to grow very fast. However, there is much trade which the GATT either does not cover, for example services, or does not cover well enough, for example agriculture and textiles. The main problem in world trade at the moment is the EC's agricultural policy. Farmers are paid subsidies according to the amount they grow, and are often guaranteed certain prices for the sale of their produce. As a result, farmers grow too much (overproduction) and the price of agricultural products falls around the world, hurting countries that export agricultural products, as well as EC consumers and taxpayers who subsidize the scheme.

In 1990 the price of lamb fell because of overproduction. As a result, French farmers lost money and organized violent protests against imports of foreign lamb. In the same year British cattle were affected by BSE or 'mad cow disease' and there were fears that the disease could be passed on to humans.

58

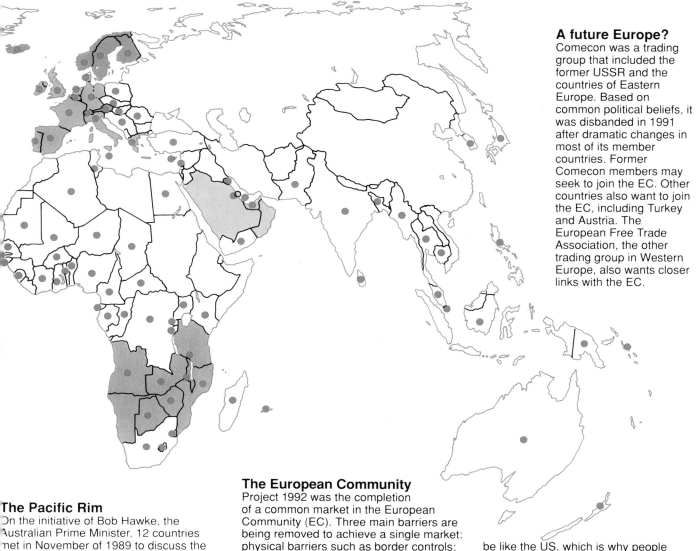

A future Europe?

Comecon was a trading group that included the former USSR and the countries of Eastern Europe. Based on common political beliefs, it was disbanded in 1991 after dramatic changes in most of its member countries. Former Comecon members may seek to join the EC. Other countries also want to join the EC, including Turkey and Austria. The European Free Trade Association, the other trading group in Western Europe, also wants closer links with the EC.

The Pacific Rim

On the initiative of Bob Hawke, the Australian Prime Minister, 12 countries met in November of 1989 to discuss the creation of a Pacific Rim trading group. Although this has not yet come about, with the US and Japan as members, as well as the fastest growing economies in the world, such a group could potentially rival the EC.

Pacific Rim: potential members

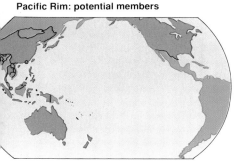

Percentage shares of world trade

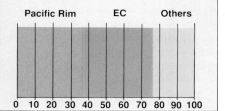

The European Community

Project 1992 was the completion of a common market in the European Community (EC). Three main barriers are being removed to achieve a single market: physical barriers such as border controls; technical barriers such as different national standards for products; and tax barriers such as different national rates of VAT (sales tax). There are proposals for the economies of EC members to be more closely linked, which would involve a central European bank and a single currency for Europe. The EC would then be like the US, which is why people sometimes talk of 'the United States of Europe'. Not all EC members agree about how far the union should go. The EC is set up to benefit its members, and some countries, including the US, have complained that the EC is building a 'Fortress Europe' with free trade inside but protection from outside invasion.

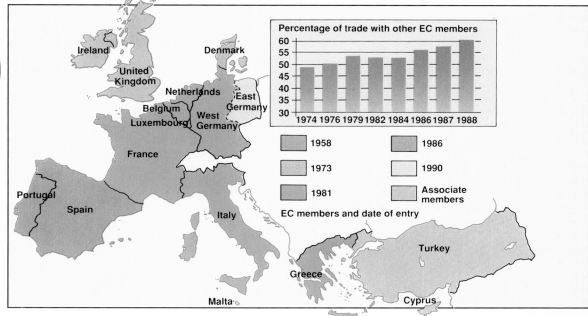

Percentage of trade with other EC members

EC members and date of entry

1958
1973
1981
1986
1990
Associate members

28 Foreign Investment

The last three decades have seen a big increase in the number of multinational corporations, or companies with enterprises located in more than one country. International takeovers (one company buying another company) have led to a reduction in the number of businesses in certain sectors. But the surviving businesses have become bigger and bigger. As a result, out of the world's largest 100 economic units, 53 are countries, while 47 are multinational corporations. The expansion of multinational production means that the same type of product is made in more countries than ever before and that an individual product may be the result of work done in several countries.

The ability to shift activity around the globe puts large corporations in a powerful position. Governments often have to offer incentives for them to locate facilities in their country.

The world car

Cars are now produced or assembled in over 50 countries, sometimes by special licensing with large foreign companies. In the 1980s Ford announced that their new Escort model would be a 'World Car,' assembled in 2 locations from parts made in 15 countries. Such strategies allow the company to diversify its operations, but also mean that if there is a strike in any one plant it can quickly stop production in other countries.

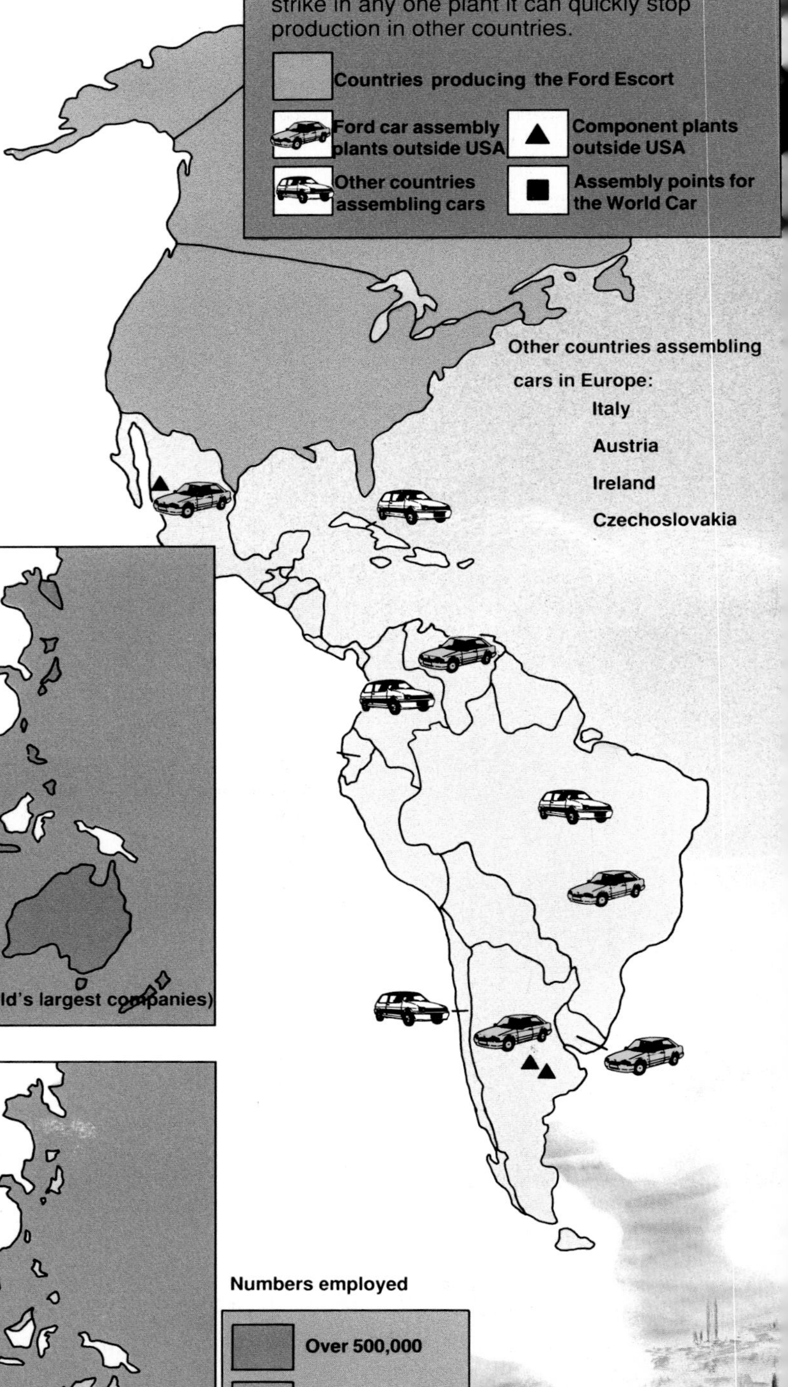

	Countries producing the Ford Escort

	Ford car assembly plants outside USA	▲	Component plants outside USA
	Other countries assembling cars	■	Assembly points for the World Car

Other countries assembling cars in Europe:
Italy
Austria
Ireland
Czechoslovakia

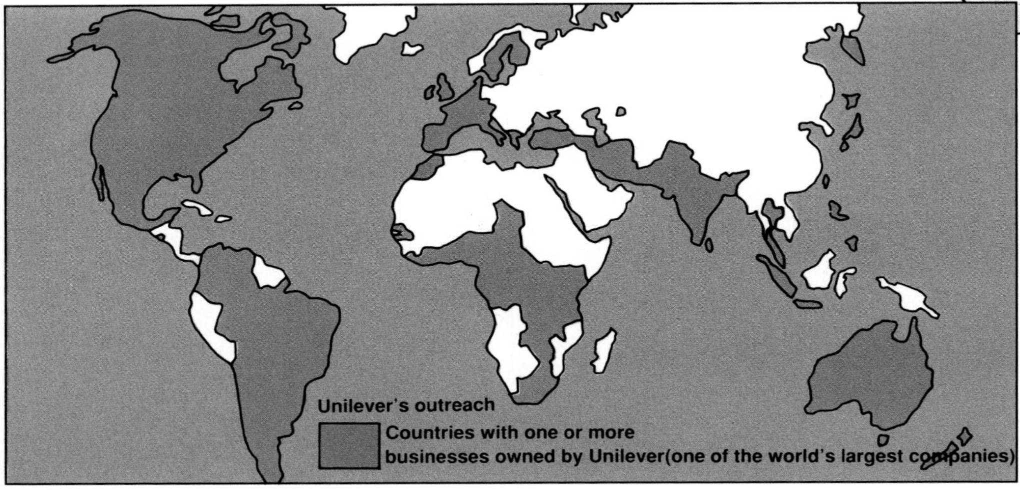

Unilever's outreach

	Countries with one or more businesses owned by Unilever(one of the world's largest companies)

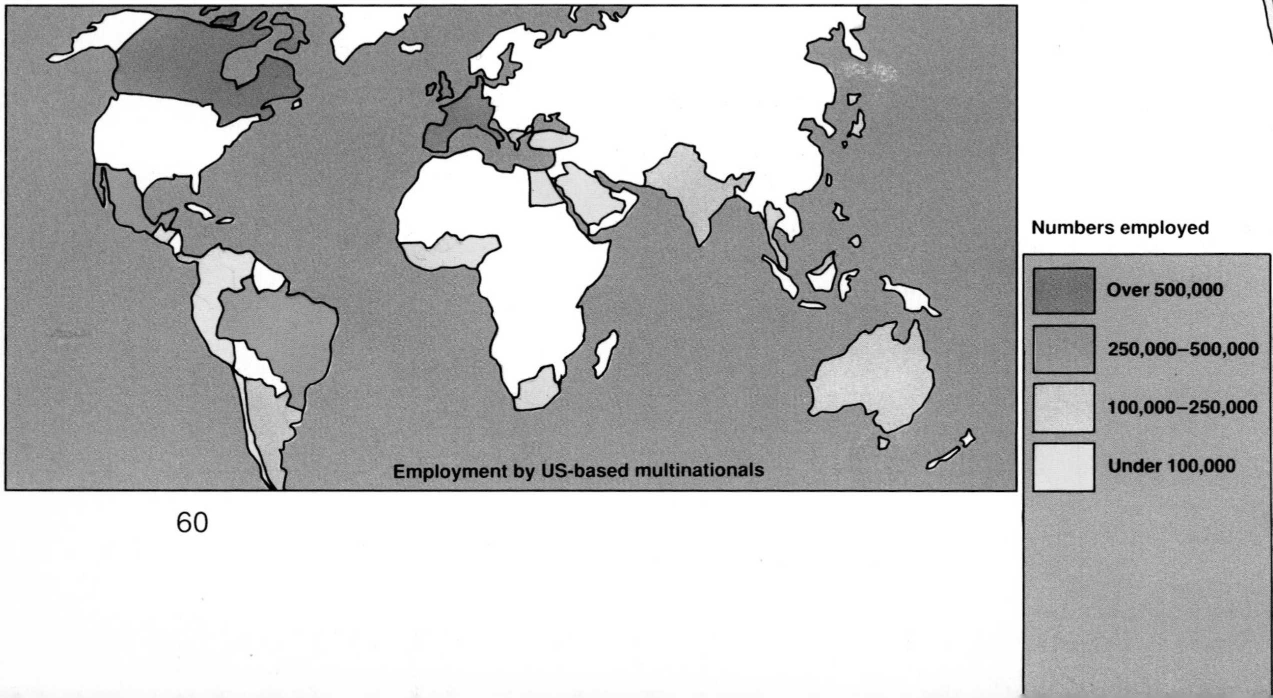

Employment by US-based multinationals

Numbers employed

	Over 500,000
	250,000–500,000
	100,000–250,000
	Under 100,000

'Free Trade Zones' or 'Export-Processing Zones' in Asia

▲ 14 zones in Singapore

SAARLOUIS

Japanese investment

Because Japan's exports to Europe far exceed its imports from that continent, the country is under pressure to reduce them. One strategy adopted in recent years has been for Japanese companies to locate within Europe itself. The UK is an attractive destination, since it has cheap skilled labor, good labor relations, and workers who speak Japan's first foreign language – English. In addition, government grants to locate in declining regions reduce initial costs. When the Nissan car company was looking for a good location for an assembly plant, Britain offered $180m and won. Nissan built its plant on Tyneside.

Free Trade Zones

To attract outside investment a number of governments have created Free Trade Zones. Firms moving into them may be given tax concessions, freedom from customs controls, the right to take profits back home, ready-made roads or buildings, and supplies of cheap labour. FTZs employ a million workers worldwide, but critics argue that work conditions are exploitative. Once the incentives end, there is often nothing to keep firms from leaving. This fate befell one of the early schemes: Mexico's Border Industrialization Program in the 1970s.

The US chemicals grab

Low profits and a stagnant domestic market encouraged European chemicals companies to buy businesses in the USA, taking advantage of the weak US dollar. In 1986 there were 177 such purchases, and now foreign companies own one fifth of the US chemicals industry (an investment worth $26.5 billion in 1987). A large internal market and much research and development expertise mean that such strategies should revive dwindling profits. Hoescht, the German firm, became the world's largest chemicals producer through expansion in the US. Not used to foreign owners, the speed and scale of the takeovers worried the US industry.

Foreign direct investment in US chemicals (by country of origin)
Netherlands 25.4%
W. Germany 20.3%
Britain 21.7%
France 11.3%
Switzerland 9%
Japan 1.5%
Canada 1%
Other 9.8%

61

Glossary

Budget deficit The amount by which government spending exceeds income.

Centrally planned economy A system where production throughout the economy is coordinated by the government.

Common market An arrangement between two or more countries under which trade barriers are removed.

Consumption The use of resources to meet current needs and desires.

Developed countries OECD members (see below) and the other high income countries.

Developing countries General term used to describe low and middle income countries; some low income countries are actually getting poorer and consequently are not really developing economically.

Division of labor The allocation of specialized tasks to different workers.

Economies of scale The reduction in cost per item associated with increased scale of production.

European Bank for Reconstruction and Development A new international organization responsible for facilitating the move towards free market economies in Eastern European countries.

European Community A common market consisting of 12 European countries.

Exchange rate The price or rate at which one currency is exchanged for another.

Exports Goods and services sold to another country.

Food and Agriculture Organization An agency of the United Nations, established to assist with agriculture in developing countries.

Foreign aid The transfer of resources from richer to poorer countries.

Foreign debt Money owed to a foreign lender.

Free market economy A system in which resources are allocated by supply and demand without government regulation of markets. In practice, however, some limitations are imposed on markets in all countries.

GATT (General Agreement on Tariffs and Trade) An international agreement under which member countries have agreed to reduce trade barriers.

GDP (Gross Domestic Product) The total value of all the goods and services produced in an economy in a given period (usually a year).

Germany East and West Germany were united in 1990. Where world map data in this *Atlas* refers separately to East and West Germany before their unification, a broken border line is shown.

Government budget deficit A shortfall between government revenue and spending.

GNP (Gross National Product) GDP plus income from foreign investments and less income from investments flowing abroad.

Hyperinflation A rapid rise in inflation to the point where money loses its effectiveness as a medium of exchange.

Imports Goods and services bought from another country.

Industrial relations The relationship between employer and employees.

Inflation A general increase in the level of prices.

Informal economy The largely unregulated and untaxed sector of the economy in many Third World cities; it consists of such activities as street selling and small-scale manufacturing.

Interest rate The proportion of a sum of money paid in return for a loan.

Investment Spending money on projects that will generate goods and services for future consumption.

Market An arrangement where potential sellers of a good or service make contact with potential buyers.

Market clearing The effect when the demand for a good or service is sufficient to use up the supply.

Mixed economy A market economy with both private and public ownership of economic enterprises.

Money A medium of exchange which is widely accepted as payment for goods and in the settlement of debts.

Multinational corporation A company that produces goods or services in a number of countries.

NICs (Newly Industrialized Countries) So-called because of their relatively recent and economically successful development of their own industrial sectors.

OECD (Organization for Economic Cooperation and Development) A group of 24 advanced industrial countries.

Private sector Households and businesses.

Production The use of inputs such as labor, equipment, materials and energy to produce goods and services.

Productivity The ratio of the output of goods and services to the inputs necessary to produce them.

Protection Trade policies designed to reduce imports and boost exports.

Public sector Government- and state-owned industries.

Saving Income that is not spent.

Tax Compulsory payment of money by individuals and businesses to government. Tax is usually paid on income and on purchases.

Third World Another term for developing countries – the countries of the South in the world's North–South divide.

Trade deficit The amount by which the cost of imports exceeds the value of exports.

Trade unions Organizations set up to further the interests of workers.

Unemployment The existence of people who want to work, but are unable to find a job.

USSR (Union of Soviet Socialist Republics) Following the failed attempt to remove its leader, Mikhail Gorbachev, in 1991, the USSR was reorganized into a collection of independent republics. All of the data in this *Atlas* apply to the USSR before its reorganization.

Welfare state The provision by government of education, health and welfare services, paid for through taxation.

World Bank An international organization set up to promote economic development.

Index